Here Be Dragons

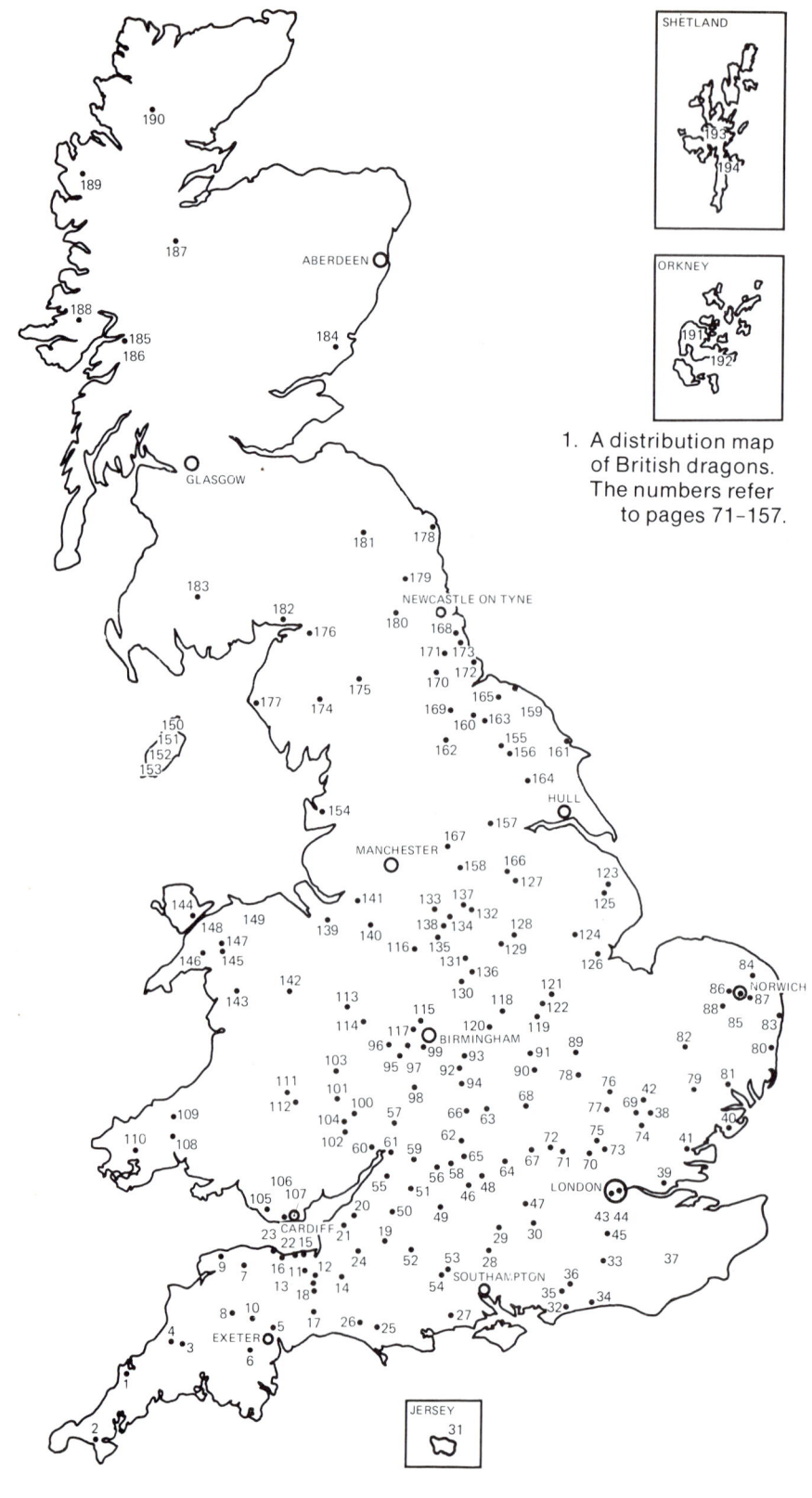

1. A distribution map of British dragons. The numbers refer to pages 71–157.

Here Be Dragons

RALPH WHITLOCK

London
GEORGE ALLEN & UNWIN
Boston   Sydney

George Allen & Unwin (Publishers) Ltd,
40 Museum Street, London WC1A 1LU, UK

George Allen & Unwin (Publishers) Ltd,
Park Lane, Hemel Hempstead, Herts HP2 4TE, UK

Allen & Unwin Inc.,
9 Winchester Terrace, Winchester, Mass 01890, USA

George Allen & Unwin Australia Pty Ltd,
8 Napier Street, North Sydney, NSW 2060, Australia

First published in 1983

British Library Cataloguing in Publication Data

Whitlock, Ralph
    Here be dragons.
1. Dragons
I. Title
398'.469'025941   GR830.D7
ISBN 0–04–398007–4

Set in 11 on 13 point Bembo by V & M Graphics Ltd, Aylesbury, Bucks.
and printed in Great Britain
by William Clowes Limited, Beccles and London

Contents

Illustrations

7

Preface

The scope for dragon-hunters in Britain is greater than might be expected. The following pages list over 190 places where dragons are or have been found, and I am by no means sure that I have located them all. New discoveries probably await the assiduous searcher. It is a quest which could enliven holidays for many a year, and I would be interested to hear of any other dragons which are brought to light; please write to me c/o the publishers.

Hobby horses are borderline cases in a book on dragons. They are included largely because Snap, the Norwich dragon **(85)**, though always referred to as a dragon, is obviously also a hobby horse. The transition from hobby horse to dragon, or vice versa, is perhaps explained by the reference in a Lancashire record to 'the dragon with the head of a horse'. A dragon's head, as portrayed in many a picture and sculpture, does indeed resemble that of a horse. It would seem, too, that the name 'dragon' was often applied, no doubt by disapproving Christian priests, to images of ancient gods who may have had the heads of rams, bulls, horses or some other animal. I have therefore included in this book the more important and best-known hobby horses, and examples of some of the others.

The figures in bold type are cross-references (by dragon number) to the Gazetteer between pages 71 and 157.

RALPH WHITLOCK

Introduction

WHY DRAGONS?

The simple answer to that question is that dragons are very satisfactory characters to have around, provided it is someone else who encounters them, not oneself. In many respects we are all children at heart, and children love blood-curdling stories. What child has not been thrilled by Red Riding Hood and the Big Bad Wolf, by the child-eating witch in *Hansel and Gretel,* by *The Three Little Pigs* and by the bloodthirsty goings-on in *Three Blind Mice*? You cannot, in any case, have a rip-roaring fight without a villain. The hero has to have a worthwhile antagonist, and what could be more satisfactory than a fire-breathing dragon? Yet, although it is good to know that Red Riding Hood escapes and that Hansel and Gretel are not eaten by the witch, we feel some sympathy with the wolf and the witch who, after all, have made the stories possible. We can understand the popularity of Snap, with smoke and flames coming out of his nostrils and ears, as he capered among the crowds in the streets of Norwich (**85**). The children shrieked and the girls scuttled away, but when he was eventually pensioned off and retired to the Museum, the parade can hardly have seemed the same without him.

The dragons of mediaeval drama and folklore therefore existed on their own merits. We might enquire today where they came from and how they happened to be there, but for our ancestors it was enough that they were integral parts of the play and of local tradition, which would have seemed somewhat emasculated without them.

Serpent worship
It will be seen from pages 32–53 that in almost every culture a serpent or

11

sea monster occupies a prominent place in the pantheon of gods. In Mesopotamia, Tiamat, the mother of all living things, now lives on as a huge sea-serpent in the stormy ocean. In ancient Egypt the sun is daily chased across the sky by Apep, the serpent-dragon, eager to devour it. Ananta, the serpent-dragon of ancient India, is the counterpart of the Sumerian Tiamat. The adversary of the Canaanite god Baal was Lotan, the crooked or primeval serpent. In Greek mythology Gaea, the mother of the gods, also produced a brood of serpents and dragons by promiscuously mating with Tartarus, the god of the Underworld.

The Serpent of Midgard and the other monsters of Norse mythology are destined to play a leading role in the apocalyptic disasters which will culminate in the destruction of the world, and this grim northern vision bears a startling resemblance to that of St John in the Book of Revelation. In both there is war in heaven, with cataclysmic consequences.

Dr William Stukeley, who in the early eighteenth century was one of the first antiquaries to visit and write about Avebury (**49**), considered the ground plan of that massive megalithic monument to represent a solar serpent, the Sanctuary being the head, the winding avenues the neck and tail and the great circle the coiled body. He may have been right. Oddly, perhaps significantly, on the twelfth-century font in Avebury church is a carving of a battle between a winged serpent and a bishop. The serpent is biting the bishop's foot, while the bishop is hitting at it with his crozier.

Pagan versus Christian

That carving in Avebury church, and the parallels with the Book of Revelation, remind us that, during the long period when dragon stories took root and developed, the Christian religion was engaged in an arduous struggle with its predecessors. As well as the Norse and Anglo-Saxons, with their allegiance to Woden, Thor and other deities, there were more ancient religions which still had a strong grip on the illiterate peasantry. It seems probable that the lore attached to at least some of these primitive attempts to explain the universe contained a strong element of serpent worship. Indeed, in view of the virtual universality of the theme, it would be surprising if it had not.

Biblical references to the downfall of the serpent in Eden and to St Michael prevailing over 'that old serpent', the Devil, therefore took on a new significance in Christianity's fight against the pagan religions, and one can imagine energetic priests fostering their local dragon stories, embellishing them with extraneous details from the classics and turning them to the Church's advantage. Several British dragon stories probably originated as allegories, illustrating a local confrontation between the adherents of the two religions. The story of the Crowcombe worm (**11**) may well contain submerged history of that sort. So may those of the Mordiford dragon (**100**), the Wherwell cockatrice (**28**), the Ludham dragon (**84**), the Handale dragon (**159**), the Strathmartin dragon (**184**) and a number of others.

The outstanding example of the Christian Church taking on itself the reflected glory of a courageous dragon-killer is seen in the story of St George and the dragon. The cult of St George was introduced to Western Europe by the Crusaders, and he was a very satisfactory soldier-saint for those formidable warriors. Reputedly he lived in Palestine in the third century AD and was a high-ranking officer in the Roman Army. When the Emperor Diocletian began a severe persecution of Christians in 303, George found the courage to remonstrate with him but paid for the intervention with his life.

It is not until nearly a thousand years later that we hear anything about the dragon, when it appears in a thirteenth-century book about the saints. The dragon seems to have been a swamp monster, perhaps a crocodile, living near a place named Silene which some authorities located in Libya, others near Beirut. The dragon followed the usual programme of starting on an innocuous diet, then moving on to sheep and finally demanding a maiden a day. For a time the victims were chosen by lot, but eventually, the supply of maidens being nearly exhausted, it was the king's daughter's turn. The king argued and procrastinated, but at last the time came when the princess was bound fast to a rock, awaiting the arrival of the dragon.

Providentially George, a wandering knight, arrived first. After enquiring how she came to be in that plight, he remounted his horse and prepared to do battle with the monster. In some versions of the story he slays the dragon after a furious fight; in others he so subdues it that the fearsome creature allows itself to be led into the city, where the citizens kill it. This second version is a bit of religious propaganda, however, for George will only allow the dragon to be killed if the people will consent to become Christians. It nevertheless parallels the story of St Carantoc of Carhampton (**16**).

The princess tended to be discreetly eliminated by those who in the Middle Ages adopted the story of St George as a suitable subject for the

Victoria and Albert Museum

2. The cult of St George and the dragon was introduced to western Europe by the Crusaders. Here the battle is depicted on a Spanish altar-piece.

pictures, sculptures, wood carvings and other portrayals of the event in churches. But she explains the reference in many versions of the mumming plays to St George (or King George) killing the dragon in order to rescue 'the king of Egypt's daughter' (see pages 24–5). The same theme of a last-minute reprieve for a princess also occurs in one version of the Lyminster

14

knucker story (**32**), and there are hints of it in the tale of the Laidly Worm (**178**).

In the Bible itself, the dragon-killing champion is St Michael: 'There was war in heaven: Michael and his angels fought against the dragon; and the dragon fought and his angels, and prevailed not; neither was their place found any more in heaven. And the great dragon was cast out, that old serpent, called the Devil and Satan, which deceiveth the whole world: he was cast out into the earth, and his angels were cast out with him.' (*Book of Revelation.*) St Michael is the leader of the hosts of heaven – the supreme warrior saint to whom innumerable hill-top churches in western Europe are dedicated, evidently because serpent worship was particularly associated with high or isolated hills. Some folklorists, however, identify him with the Celtic god of light, Lugh.

Jacqueline Simpson has discovered over forty dragon-slaying saints in the Western Church, and doubtless study of the lore of Eastern Churches would add to the number. Among them is St Margaret, who was associated with the Norwich pageant. Some legends identify St Margaret with the maiden rescued by St George, but in other versions she herself is a dragon-killer, a status achieved by making the sign of the Cross in the dragon's interior after the monster had swallowed her.

EXISTING SURVIVALS

Artefacts

By far the greatest number of representations of dragons are to be found in churches. They are in the form of carvings on bench-ends, misericords and other items of ecclesiastical furniture, of stone sculptures, of paintings either framed or on walls, and of stained glass windows. Sometimes there is an association with a local story; sometimes not. A favourite theme is of St George, though sometimes St Michael or another saint, killing a dragon.

Some dragons have been moved from churches to museums. Examples are the Wherwell cockatrice (**28**), which was once a weather-vane on Wherwell Priory and is now in Andover Museum, and the carved capital (one of the oldest portrayals of dragons in England) from the Abbey Church, Reading, which has found its way into Reading Museum (**47**). In Durham Cathedral can be seen the sword with which an intrepid knight slew the Sockburn worm (**169**) at a crossing of the river Tees. The spear

Bridgeman Art Library

The Dean and Chapter of Durham

3 (left). In the Bible the dragon-killing champion is St Michael. This painting is by Bartolomeo Bermejo of Barcelona.

4 (right). The Conyers falchion, with which the Sockburn worm (**169**) was slain at a crossing of the river Tees, can be seen in Durham Cathedral.

with which gallant John of Aller killed the Aller dragon (**14**) is not now in the church of the little Somerset village of Aller but resides in the neighbouring church of Low Ham.

The Bisterne dragon (**27**) is depicted in sculpture over the door of Bisterne Park, while stone effigies of the dogs which assisted in its killing stand guard at either end of the terrace in the gardens. A huge boulder, known as the Spindle Stone, near Bamburgh Castle, Northumberland, is pointed out as the stone to which the hero tethered his horse when he went to do battle with the Laidly Worm (**178**). Visitors to Lambton Castle, in county Durham, may see a statue of Lord Lambton in spiky armour in the act of killing the Lambton dragon or worm (**168**), and they also used to be able to inspect the stone trough from which the monster drank its tribute of milk in the early days before it became savage.

Norwich Museum, in the Castle Keep, houses the last Norwich Snap (**85**), which was made about 1795 and appeared in procession in the city streets from time to time until 1850. A second Snap, from the Pockthorpe area of Norwich (**87**), may also be seen there. The Salisbury Hob-nob (**53**), if it can be accepted as a dragon, resides in Salisbury Museum.

Documents

In the absence of the Press in the centuries in question, the nearest we can get to authentic reporting (and who would dream of doubting the authenticity of what they read in the Press?) are the accounts of such historians as Matthew of Westminster, Roger de Hoveden, the authors of the *Anglo-Saxon Chronicle*, Mallet and Holinshed. They are among the sources of the following dated references to dragons in surviving documents.

AD 497. A star of marvellous size and brilliancy appeared, shining in one single ray, attached to which ray was extended a ball of fire in the shape of a dragon, and out of its mouth proceeded two rays.

793. Dreadful prodigies alarmed the wretched nation of the English; for terrific lightnings and dragons in the air and strokes of fire were seen hovering on high, and shooting to and fro, which were ominous signs of the great famine and the frightful and ineffable slaughter of multitudes of men which ensued.

795. Fearful lightnings and dragons blazing in a dreadful manner were seen to fly through the air, signs which foreshadowed a mighty famine.

1066. A dragon was seen in the sky at the time when King Harold was killed at the battle of Hastings (doubtless Halley's Comet).

1170. In the seventeenth year of Henry II, there was seen at St Osythes (Essex – **40**) a dragon of marvellous bigness, which, by moving, burned houses.

1177. In this year many dragons were seen in England. The same year a great wind blew up shortly before Christ's Nativity, and the sun eclipsed.

1221. During a violent tempest fiery dragons and flying spirits were seen in the air.

1222. In this year there were tumultuous riots in the city of London. Dragons were seen flying through the air.

1233. Terrible bloodshed and a generall trouble throughout England, Wales and Ireland. About the same time, to wit, in June, in the south part of England neere to the sea coast, two huge dragons appeared fighting in the aire, and after a long fight the one overcam the other, and followed him, fleeing into the depth of the sea, and so they were seen no more....Moreover in this yeare great variance and strife arose betwixt the king and his barons.

1274. In the vigil of St Nicholas there was an earthquake and thunder and lightning; a fiery dragon and a comet terrified the English.

1395. In Aprill, there was seene a fierce dragon in manie places of England; which dreadful sight as it made manie a one amazed, so it ministred occasion of mistrust to the minds of the marvellous, that some great mischeefe was imminent....A certain thing appeared in the likeness of fire in many parts of England, now of one fashion, now of another, as it were every night, but yet in divers places all November and December. This fiery apparition oftentimes when anybody went alone it would go with him, and would stand still when he stood still. To some it appeared in the likeness of a turning wheel burning; to other some round in the likeness of a barrel, flashing out flames of fire at the head; to some other in the likeness of a long burning lance; and so to divers folks, at divers times and seasons, it showed itself in divers forms and fashions a great part of winter, especially in Leicestershire and Northamptonshire; and when many went together it approached not near them, but appeared to them as it were afar off.

1532. In manye countries were dragons crowned seene flying by flocks or companies in the ayre, having swines snowtes; and sometimes there were seen foure hundred flying together in a companie.

Heraldry

Dragons occur on numerous crests and armorial bearings, often, though not always, associated with a dragon-killing story. The Venables crest, for instance, shows a dragon with a child in its jaws, commemorating the occasion when Sir Thomas Venables, seeing a dragon seizing and about to swallow a child at the edge of a pool, shot the monster in the eye with an arrow (**140**). And did you know that Oliver Cromwell had a coat of arms prepared for himself and chose a dragon as one of its supporters? Even Joshua, in a fourteenth-century French painting of Old Testament figures, is shown as a knight with a dragon emblazoned on his shield.

Heraldry developed in Europe in the twelfth century. It was apparently unknown at the time of the Norman Conquest of England but was common throughout Europe by the thirteenth century. Its introduction and evolution therefore coincided with the Crusaders, though what the links may have been is obscure. Certainly it quickly followed the introduction of visors to helmets. With a visor covering his face a knight was anonymous, and the bearing of some device on his shield or on a banner attached to his lance was a useful, even essential, means of identification.

The term 'coat of arms' refers strictly to the devices on a shield. The armorial bearings, which are properly called the 'heraldic achievement', include also the helmet, the mantling (a cloth suspended from the top of the helmet and allowed to hang down over the back of the wearer), the crest, the wreath (which fastens the crest to the helmet), the motto, the supporters and a few other accessories. Dragons in heraldry usually feature as supporters, like the lion and the unicorn, though they sometimes appear on the shields.

Although heraldry as such does not make its appearance until early mediaeval times, some of the devices used on coats of arms have a much greater antiquity. In his splendid book, *Heraldry, Sources, Symbols and Meaning*, Ottfried Neubecker asserts: 'The important charges – the cross, the lily, the eagle, the lion and the dragon – reach back into the mists of the past. It was logical that they should become the marks of royalty, for they had been this before the emergence of heraldic arms.'

As supporters of coats of arms, dragons certainly had many royal and other important associations. During the reigns of the later Tudors – Edward VI, Mary and Elizabeth I – the Welsh dragon was one of the supporters of the royal arms of England, the other being the English lion. A dragon appears as a crest on the arms of the kingdom of Aragon in the second half of the fourteenth century and somewhat earlier as a crest on the arms of Brabant and on the arms of the English Earls of Lancaster. The supporters of the coat of arms of Henry VI were a red dragon and a white hound. François I of France had on his coat of arms a special sort of dragon,

Barnabys Picture Library

5. Dragons on inn signs are borrowed from heraldry. This is the sign of the
Green Dragon Inn near Barnet, Hertfordshire.

a salamander, a creature whose natural element was said to be fire. Sir
Francis Drake, appropriately, carried a dragon on his coat of arms
although, as was befitting for a West Country man, his dragon was a
wyvern. Two red dragons, with a pattern of golden roses on their wings,
are the official supporters of the arms of Carlisle.

In heraldry, as in church carvings, dragons are for no obvious reason
often associated with panthers, which may be either black or spotted.

The dragons which feature on inn signs are borrowed from heraldry.
The Green Dragon is probably the commonest. There are Green Dragons
at Carlisle, Exeter, Marlborough, Downend (Bristol), Alderbury
(Salisbury) and Flaunden (Hertfordshire), and readers will find many

6. The Uffington White Horse (**46**) could as easily be a dragon as a horse and has a Dragon Hill at its approach from the road.

others. There is a Red Dragon at Bridgend (Glamorgan) and a Dragon (colour unspecified) at Harrogate.

Landscape

When looking for dragons at prehistoric sites the dragon-hunter usually has to be content with the site itself, though the Uffington White Horse (**46**) is exceptionally rewarding in that it offers not only a Dragon Hill but also a blowing stone which may well be the authentic voice of the horse or dragon god of the tribe which once occupied the Vale. At Avebury (**49**) one can trace the alleged outline of the dragon or serpent from the Sanctuary, around the great circle (which is said to represent its coiled body) and so to the tip of its tail, marked by a cluster of stones on Beckhampton Down. In other places, as at Bignor Hill in Sussex (**35**), the eye of faith can discern the great spirals around a hill where a dragon is said to have coiled its massive body. Some dragons are associated with tumuli which are reputed to hold treasure, the dragons being the guardians of the hoard.

At Wherwell a plot of land, exactly four acres in extent, which was offered as a reward to whoever would kill the Wherwell cockatrice (**28**), is still identified in Harewood Forest. It is known as Green's Acres, after the hero who slew the monster and who was a serving-man of the Priory, named Green.

A link has been suggested between dragon worship, or serpent worship, and the mazes which once existed on numerous British sites. Some still survive, as at Saffron Walden (Essex), Wing (Rutland) and St Agnes (Scilly Isles). Many of them were cut in turf, often on hill-tops or hillsides, and the association of so many of them with tumuli nearby cannot be pure chance. Where the actual mazes have been destroyed their former sites may be established by local place-names (Mizmaze and Troy Town are examples) or by local traditions or memories. The mazes were usually circular or spiral, resembling a coiled serpent, and some of them were the venues of spiralling dances associated with such festivals as May Day or Midsummer.

Behaviour

Records exist of behaviour patterns arising from dragon legends and surviving at least until the nineteenth century. For example, at Bamburgh Castle local girls were afraid to venture near the beach lest they should see the monstrous toad which derived its existence from the tale of the Laidly Worm (**178**). They feared that, like the princess who was transformed into the worm and like the wicked stepmother who became the toad, they too would be robbed of their beauty.

At Wherwell (**28**) it was known that the cockatrice was hatched by a toad from a duck's egg and, until recently at least, no inhabitant of Wherwell could be persuaded to eat a duck's egg!

The sequel to the story of the Mordiford dragon (**100**) indicates that the legend was believed at least as late as the 1870s. That was when the Rector of Mordiford found two old women trying to drown some newts in the church font. They told him that these were dragon spawn and, if not disposed of when small, would grow to be dangerous monsters like their predecessor.

Mumming plays and hobby horses

The demarcation line between dragons and hobby horses is decidedly blurred. There is little real difference between Snap, of Norwich (**85**), which is definitely a dragon, and the Padstow obby oss (**1**) which claims, without much conviction, to be a horse. The dragon-hunter need therefore not feel that he is cheating if he takes note of the pageants and parades in which hobby horses appear or used to appear. Though dragons themselves seldom feature in the performances of mumming plays, hobby horses sometimes do, and dragons are often mentioned in the script, usually when St George is speaking of the feats he has already performed. Incidentally, mumming plays are always well worth watching!

Dragons were meant to be killed. Much of their popularity undoubtedly derived from the dramatic possibilities of that climax to their career. Even today the prospect of participating in or witnessing a good fight can send adrenalin coursing through our bodies. Certainly few men would find any difficulty in identifying themselves with the hero of a play who fought with and slew a dragon – that is, assuming they could bring themselves to believe that such a creature existed. Whether, in this liberated age, women would similarly identify themselves with the maiden destined to be rescued from the dragon's claws I would hesitate to say.

Conflict is the essence of good drama. A glorious fight (or, in some instances, several fights) is the focus of all extant mumming plays, which are among the oldest surviving examples of folk drama. The hero, who is the champion of light, the 'goodie' of contemporary Westerns, takes on the representative of the powers of darkness, the 'baddie'. In many versions of the plays he loses the first fight and is slain, but is duly restored to life by a 'doctor' by means of magic medicine, and so he triumphs after all. In some versions, however, the plot is complicated by the evil character being killed and raised to life again. Mumming plays being normally associated with Christmas, the period of the winter solstice, the sequence of events is generally supposed to portray the increasing dominance of the dark days of winter over the receding sun until the threat is averted by the intervention of the possessors of powerful magic, who are able to bring back to life again the dead realm of nature.

Shirley Toulson traces their origin back to the ancient midwinter sacrifice of the divine priest-king who represented the sun-god in pagan religions and who had to be slain to ensure the welfare of his people. His death could be postponed for a further year if he was able to prove his unabated strength and skill in the annual contest with a challenger.

It is perhaps because of lingering folk-memories that men were involved rather than beasts or monsters that dragons do not appear more frequently in the mumming plays, for a conventional dragon would seem to be an ideal personification of evil. In surviving versions of the plays dragons seldom appear but are often alluded to. In the Quidhampton (Salisbury) play (**54**), a character named Bold Soldier boasts:

> ''Tis I that fought the fiery dragon
> And brought him to his slaughter,
> And by that means I won
> The King of Egypt's daughter.'

In the Yateley (Hampshire) play very similar words are put into the mouth of King George:

> 'In comes I, King George, the man of courage bold,
> With this broad sword and spear I won ten crowns of gold.
> It was me who fought that fiery dragon and drove him
>   to be slaughtered,
> And by means of that I won the King of Egypt's daughter.'

A similar speech was recited by King George in a mumming play still being performed in Berkshire in 1910.

The Burford (Oxfordshire) mumming play (**62**) actually includes a fight between St George and the dragon, possibly because an effigy of a dragon was a prized possession of the town (or perhaps it was a prized possession because it was a favourite character in the play – who knows?). St George's speech, when he makes his entrance, runs:

> 'Here am I, St George,
> From Britain did I spring,
> And I will fight the fiery Dragon
> My wonders to begin.
> I'll clip his wings,
> He shall not fly;
> I'll cut him down,
> Or else I die.'

The dragon then enters and makes a speech:

24

'Who is he that seeks the Dragon's blood?
And speaks so angry and so loud?
That English dog, will he before me stand?
I'll cut him down with my courageous hand.
With my long teeth and scurvy jaws
Of such I break up half a score,
Then stay my stomach till I have more.'

The two then fight. St George falls with a mortal wound, but fortunately the doctor is at hand with a magic pill. Soon St George is on his feet again, ready to renew the battle. This time he wins. The dragon falls dying, and St George recites the victory oration:

'Here am I, St George, that worthy champion bold,
And with my sword and spear I won three crowns of gold.
I fought the fiery dragon and brought him to the slaughter,
And by that I won fair Sabra, the King of Egypt's daughter.'

For good measure, St George subsequently fights a Turkish knight and a giant.

The wording of the speech is so similar to Quidhampton and Yateley that one wonders whether the Burford play may not represent an original version, with the dragon as a participant. Possibly in the other two versions quoted the technique of making a dragon was lost and so the mummers settled for human characters.

The Burford dragon, incidentally, did not confine his appearances to mumming play performances. He was carried in procession at Whitsuntide and also on St John the Baptist's Day, the town's patronal festival. William Camden, the Elizabethan author of *Britannia*, mentions the dragon and says that it commemorated a battle between the West Saxons and the Mercians in the eighth century.

Bishop's Stortford (Hertfordshire – **74**) had a play about St Michael and the dragon, the dragon being a home-made effigy which was very popular in the town and was much in demand by neighbouring parishes, who evidently also performed dragon plays.

In Somerset C. H. Poole, who collected material during the 1870s, states: 'Mumming...consists of persons concealing their appearance and performing a drama which embodies the time-honoured legend of St George and the dragon, with many whimsical adjuncts...' But the only Somerset

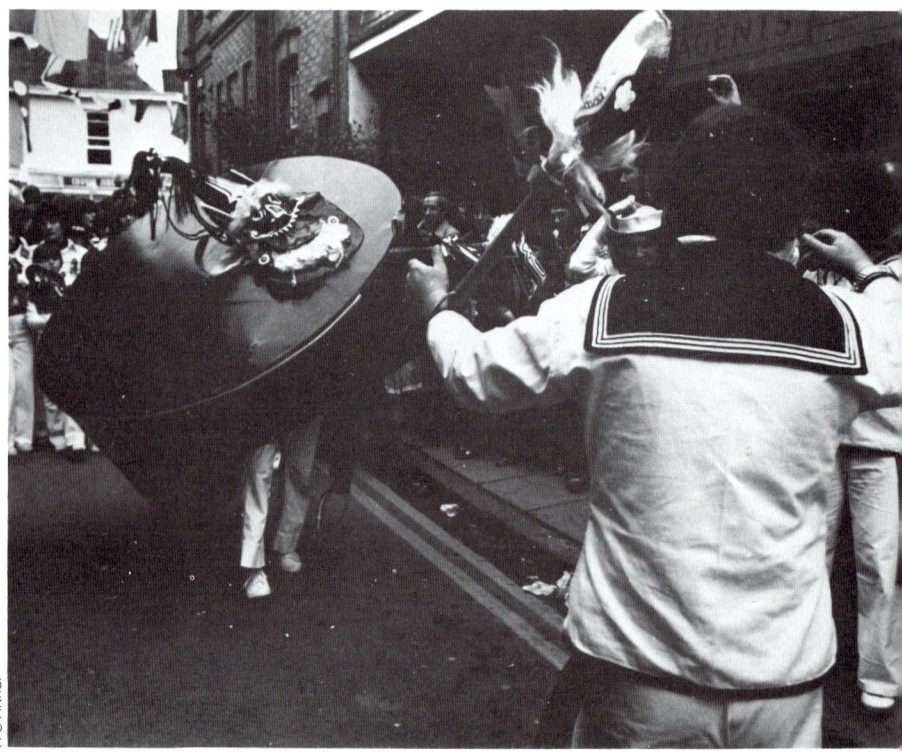

A C Arthur

7. The Padstow oss (**1**), parading through the streets of Padstow on May Day led by its Teaser, bears little resemblance to a horse but is more nearly related to Snap, the Norwich dragon.

mumming play script of which I have any knowledge – set down in 1899 though last performed, in the Castle Cary district, much earlier – makes no mention of a dragon. The battle is between St George and a Turkish knight.

The central theme of the mumming plays is death and rebirth. It occurs also in the pageant of the Padstow oss (**1**) which bears very little resemblance to a horse but is much more nearly related to Snap, the Norwich dragon. An essential part of the May Day parade in which the oss participates is that, as it prances through the streets, it collapses from time to time, apparently dying. Thereupon its attendant, the Teaser, strikes it lightly with a club (perhaps once a magic wand) and the oss springs to life again and continues its merry career.

Another feature of the programme was the endeavours of the oss to catch any girls it met. It would try to drag them under its skirts, from which they would escape liberally decorated with soot and with the promise that they

26

would have a baby within a year – obviously the relics of a fertility rite, but also drama in its widest sense. The play takes place not within the confines of a theatre stage but against the background of the whole wide countryside. There is unlimited audience participation. Yet the characters are well established and the action clearly defined.

The similar pageant at Minehead (**23**), also on or around May Day, lacks the incidents of the oss dying and being revived, as did the obsolete one at Combe Martin (**9**). On this evidence, the Padstow oss is the oldest, thus providing an answer to an ancient controversy as to which town stole the idea from the other. It is possible, however, that originally the Minehead and Combe Martin plays contained the same elements but that they have been forgotten.

The soul-caking play of Cheshire, performed on All Souls' Day in a group of villages around Antrobus, Great Budworth and Comberbatch, follows quite closely the theme of the mumming plays. There is a combat between King George and the Black Prince, who is killed and restored to life by a comic doctor. The most popular character, however, is the Wild Horse or Hodening Horse (**141**), who creates a lot of boisterous fun and horse play, though it is quite incidental to the plot. This horse is unmistakeably a horse, for its head is fashioned from a horse's skull (with sundry refinements, such as a device for making its jaws clatter and snap). We remember, however, that such a horse has been described as 'the dragon with the head of a horse'.

A curious sidelight on the cult of the Wild Horse is the tradition, in some Cheshire villages, that the skull had to be secretly buried after each performance. There seems also to have been a tradition among the villages of stealing the neighbours' horse.

The somewhat similar Hooden Horse of Kent (**37**) was apparently not originally associated with any formal play, though it has since been incorporated into one. Accounts of its performances in the nineteenth century (the last recorded one was in 1908) speak of a team of from four to eight men going from house to house on Christmas Eve and performing a set routine. The horse had a wooden head, with hinged jaw, and was carried on a pole by a bearer who was concealed by a cloth. Several of the team played musical instruments, such as an accordion or a fiddle, and one man, dressed as a woman, carried a broom. One man was the Jockey, who tried in vain to mount the horse, which indulged in any capers it could think of. Either the horse or the woman attendant chased any girls who appeared, which may or may not be significant.

The antics of the Hooden Horse resembled those of the Mari Lwyd, of South Wales, in the same period. Here, too, a party of players took the horse from house to house. The chief characters of the team were Punch and Judy, and Judy carried a broom, as did the female character in Kent. While the song in the Kent performance was incidental, in South Wales it was an essential part of the play and was in the form of a dialogue, one verse being sung by the performers outside the door and the next, as a response, by the inhabitants of the house. Apparently if the residents failed to remember the proper response, the performers were allowed to enter the house, where Judy got busy with her broom on the hearth and made a shocking mess. The tune and some of the verses survive.

In the Pembrokeshire version of the Mari Lwyd, the effigy bore no resemblance to a horse but was a sharp-snouted animal with a canvas-covered body large enough for a man to crouch inside. Just how it fitted into the conventional programme is not known. It was last seen in about 1840.

A group of villages in north Derbyshire and the adjacent part of Nottinghamshire and Yorkshire had a horse ritual performed at Christmas-time. Here too the song was important, and its words and tune are remembered and recorded. The action in the performance came from a blacksmith's attempts to shoe the horse, who, of course, resisted.

At Newbold (**137**) the horse was said to have been associated with a dragon, both characters appearing in a performance by a sword-dance team, but no details survive.

In the same region an animal with a ram's head, known as the Old Tup, features in a Christmas pageant or play which bore a strong resemblance to the mumming plays. Apart from the Old Tup, the chief character is the butcher, who attempts to kill it and meets with much resistance. In one version he succeeds, but the Old Tup is restored to life by a doctor, with a bottle of magic potion. Supporting characters include Beelzebub, an old man and an old woman, and Little Devil Doubt.

A little farther east, in Lincolnshire, there is a tradition of a wooing play, in which a hobby horse usually appeared, though without taking any special part. Sometimes girls pulled a hair from his tail for good luck.

The Ooser of Dorset and the Broad of North Wiltshire and Gloucestershire were animal characters of a similar type, though in these instances they had bulls' heads. Dorset also had a group of hero plays, performed at Christmas, which feature a hobby horse. In a version performed at Bridport and Symondsbury, first a female character, known as Old Bet, is killed and restored to life by artificial respiration; then a horse, Tommy, is led in, engages in some horse play, is killed and is revived by the same means.

At Salisbury a giant, said to represent St Christopher, and a hobby horse, the Hob-nob (**53**), were the property of the Tailors' Guild and paraded through the streets on the feast day of the Tailors' patron saint, St John the Baptist (Midsummer Day). Both are now kept in the city's museum and appear in civic processions on important occasions, the hob-nob capering about on the fringes of the crowd and snapping at the spectators.

The City of London also once possessed similar hobby horses, as did Nottingham, Newcastle-on-Tyne, Leicester, Bristol, Plymouth, Coventry, Liverpool, Hereford, Berwick-on-Tweed, Wisbech, Malmesbury and a number of smaller places. A hobby horse was also associated with the Abbots Bromley horn dance, which is still performed by a team of men carrying reindeer horns.

All this consideration of hobby horses seems to take us away from the theme of dragons, were it not for the fact that the Norwich version of the hobby horse, not vastly different from others of the clan, is unequivocally termed a dragon. Snap (**85**), like the Salisbury hob-nob, was originally the property of a city guild, the Guild of St George, whose members paraded through the streets of Norwich on St George's Day, 23 April. Mediaeval documents contained frequent references to repairs to and accessories for the dragon. When the guild was suppressed, responsibility for the festivities was transferred to a St George's Company, specially created for the purpose; then from 1732 onwards, Snap became the property of Norwich Corporation. Throughout the various changes of ownership, Snap continued his merry way, cavorting about the streets when let loose on civic occasions, snapping at children and girls and collecting pennies in his gaping mouth. The last Snap effigy was made in about 1795, and it last appeared in a Norwich procession in 1850. The citizens of Norwich loved their Snap. Richard Lane, who has written a book on the subject, describes the 'Snapdragon, smoke and sparks belching from his fearsome mouth, his bat-like wings beating against his barrel-shaped body. He rushed from side to side, threatening the crowd, which revelled in his comic malevolence.'

At Mons, in Belgium, a dragon which is almost identical with Snap takes part in an annual festival on Trinity Sunday, and comparisons have naturally been made between the two, especially with a view to determining whether the Mons Lumeçon, as it is called, can throw any light on the original function of Snap. It appears that the climax of the Mons

29

event is a fight, staged in the city square, between the Lumeçon and a hero named Sir Gilles de Chin. Some authorities say the name has been corrupted and that the original reference was to a knight and his dog (*chien*). It seems that there could be a parallel here to the several British dragon-killing stories in which the hero is assisted by his dog. Was the Norwich Snap once a character in a drama with a similar theme? If so, there is no surviving record of it.

Our list of dragons includes several which, like Snap, featured in city or village pageants in the Middle Ages. In some instances a group of parishes evidently shared the expenses of making and maintaining the dragon and other properties, or sometimes one parish would take the responsibility and would let out its dragon to its neighbours for a fee. One such was Bishop's Stortford (**74**) which apparently made a practice of hiring out its dragon. Twenty-eight parishes around Royston, in Hertfordshire, used to combine to stage a play in the village of Bassingbourn (**76**), a dragon being a prominent character. Walberswick, in Suffolk (**80**), was another village which possessed a dragon effigy for use in local drama in late mediaeval times. At Leicester (**118**), a street pageant featured both St George and the dragon, in addition to a hobby horse.

Nearly all references to dragons in pageants, parades and processions belong, however, to quite late in the Middle Ages. The cult of St George did not take root in England until the time of the Crusades, and documentary mentions of dragons belong mostly to the late fifteenth and early sixteenth centuries. Even at Chester (**139**), celebrated for its Corpus Christi plays and later for its Midsummer pageants, we hear nothing of any dragon until 1498. Whether that is through lack of documentation or not is impossible to say. The earlier mystery plays were a natural development on Biblical themes of what were probably earlier traditions of street pageants and rituals, and one feels that the producers would not have ignored the dramatic possibilities of the Book of Revelation, with the dragon a prominent character, if they had been acquainted with that book. But we do not know.

The one possible allusion to earlier mediaeval drama, if it can indeed be substantiated, is to be found in the carved capital, now in Reading Museum, which once adorned the Abbey Church in Reading (**47**). Experts who have examined it closely think that a line at the junction of the head and neck of the dragons is intended to indicate that these are effigies, not real creatures. If that is so, it would seem that the eight characters (some men, some boys) who are engaged in fighting with the dragons are performing in a play.

Reading Museum & Art Gallery

8. The twelfth-century capital from the cloisters of Reading Abbey which portrays a fight between dragons and a group of men and boys (**47**).

They are fighting without weapons and attacking the monsters by the unusual method of pulling their tongues out – a horrid technique, which Jacqueline Simpson assures us is a known method of slaughtering small pigs. The human characters are also wearing strange garments, not the normal clothes of the period (about AD 1130), which may imply that they are actors dressed for the part.

A possible parallel or derivation may be found in the Chester Plays (**139**) at a much later date – 1564 – in fact, when the records speak of sixteen naked boys whose role was probably to fight with the dragon.

ORIGINS: OTHER AGES, OTHER CULTURES

Dragons once had such a worldwide distribution that their apparent extinction within the past few centuries seems similar to that of the passenger pigeon and the dodo. Not many hundreds of years ago any schoolboy from Merioneth to the Moluccas could have given a graphic description of a dragon. Indeed, many could probably do so now.

In many lands, too, schoolboys of several thousands of years ago would have been equally conversant with the appearance and behaviour of dragons. In the first pages of the earliest literature of almost every country we find references to dragons. So let us look first at some of the antecedents and probable ancestors of our familiar British dragons.

Tracing the strands of various elements in dragon stories is a fascinating study. One finds some details derived directly from Greek or Norse mythology, some from folk-memories (as with the lovely flying dragons of Penllin – **105**), some from mediaeval mystery plays, some from Biblical texts and some apparently from the remotest antiquity. Some of the tales, as we have seen, are evident allegories of the conflict between the new Christianity and the old primeval religion.

The several stories of dragons falling victims to their own appetite and eating far too large meals are paralleled by the Hittite myth of the dragon-god, Illuyankas. The heroes who allowed the dragon to swallow them and then destroyed the monster from inside have their counterparts in both Greek and Norse mythology: Jason, it will be remembered, was swallowed by a dragon when engaged in the quest for the Golden Fleece. The stories of the heroes who slay a dragon and immediately afterwards fall victim to the monster's poison come straight from the saga of Beowulf.

It is easy to see how such features could be woven into the folklore of the British countryside. Indeed, I myself, when a boy, was given an example of how a tale with an almost universal circulation could be provided with a local setting. It was related by an old villager as follows:

'Ah, now that cottage that wur pulled down when old Eli Mellish died, that wur where old Thomas Vear lived avore he. That wur avore my time. They do zay that old Thomas told a tale of how he met a man coming down White Way, wi' a oar over his shoulder. Walked up from Southampton, so er said. Man says to old Thomas, "Here, do ee know what this yer is?"

'"Aye," says Thomas, "'tis a oar, what you pushes a boat along wi'."

'"Ah well," says the man, "I can zee I got to go furder yet. I be goin' to keep goin'," her says, "till somebody says to I, 'What's that you be carr'ing then, mister?' And that's where I be goin' to stop. Somewhere where they don't know what a oar is, see. I bin a sailor fer longer than I cares to remember, and I don't want to see the sea no more."

'That's what old Thomas used to tell.'

It seemed quite a good story to me. Not till a number of years later, when my education had progressed a little farther, did I recognise it as a derivation from the classical story of Odysseus returning after his voyage from Troy. Somebody, at some time, had heard the story in this village and, in repeating it, had given it a local setting.

When the story-teller could also introduce some local topography into his account ('You can see the ridges now, where this disgusting great dragon coiled his tail round the hill!'), it clinched the authenticity of the tale.

Mesopotamia

The great dragon of Mesopotamia was Tiamat, and she was the mother of all living things, the female element of the spirit that pervades the universe.

Mansell Collection

9. This bas-relief from the palace walls at Calah (Nimrud), Assyria, and dated about 885–860 BC, shows the hero Marduk subduing Tiamat, the primeval monster who personifies chaos, darkness and evil.

Her first offspring comprised a brood of gods who, when they grew up, became so rebellious and unruly that their father made up his mind to eradicate the lot of them. Getting wind of his intentions, however, they acted first. They captured, bound and killed their father.

Tiamat, who hitherto had been on the side of her children and who had pleaded with their father for them, now turned against them. To aid her revenge, she gave birth to a monstrous brood of dragons, serpents, demons and other ferocious creatures, who forthwith set about plaguing the gods. Eventually a god-hero, Marduk, agreed to meet Tiamat in single combat. After a herculean battle in the heavens he eventually slew his mother; then, turning his attention to her clutch of monsters, he caught and massacred them as well. These deeds accomplished, he set the bounds of heaven and earth and sea, established the sun and moon in their places, and created Man to be his servant.

Such is the story related in the Creation Epic, the oldest literature of which we have any knowledge. Tiamat is depicted as an immense sea-serpent, her home being in the stormy sea. Dragons, serpents, cockatrices, crocodiles and other monsters would seem natural offspring for such a mother.

Egypt

Apep, the serpent-dragon of ancient Egypt, pursues the sun on his daily journey across the sky. All day long he is easily kept at bay, except on the rare occasions of eclipses, but at night his chance comes. Every night is marked by a deadly conflict between Apep and the champions of the sun god, Ra, the chief of whom is the god Seth. Apep is slain by a trick and is cut to pieces, and the sun rises again triumphantly when morning comes. But the chopped-up portions of Apep quickly come together again, to form a serpent-dragon as formidable as ever, in readiness for the inevitable renewal of the conflict after sunset.

In one of her aspects the great goddess Hathor, or Isis, the beneficent earth-mother, becomes a bloodthirsty, dragon-like killer, not unlike the Babylonian Tiamat.

India

Ananta, the serpent-dragon of Indian mythology, resembles Tiamat in being one of the primal forces in the creation of the universe but is regarded as one manifestation of the supreme god Vishnu. There is thus no conflict between them, and Ananta, who is apparently male, is immortal. He is

34

portrayed as a monster with many heads, sometimes nine but sometimes more.

Another Indian dragon, Vritra, is an evil monster whose home is in the clouds. It approaches the parched land on the wings of the monsoon, holding within its body vast reservoirs of water but refusing to release them until the weather god, Indra, attacks it with a bolt of lightning. Then the dragon bursts and the land is watered.

Indian legend deals, too, with a host of minor serpents or dragons, known collectively as Nagas. They had so many different forms that it is almost impossible to generalise about them. Some, like Vritra and Indra, were concerned with the weather, others with streams and rivers. Some guarded hidden treasure; others were the guardians of the palace of the gods in the heavens. Some were short-tempered and, when aroused, were capable of killing off whole populations with their poisonous breath. Some had their homes underground or at the bottom of rivers and lakes. Some were the instructors of mankind in the arts and sciences.

One of the lake-dwelling Naga kings once protected the Buddha from the fury of the elements. The Buddha, sitting on the shore of a lake, was rapt in meditation when a great storm arose. Rising from the surface of the lake, beneath which was his home, the Naga king saw the plight of the Buddha, who was of course completely oblivious to his surroundings. To protect him, the Naga wrapped his coils around the sage seven times and spread seven of his cobra-like hoods as an umbrella.

China

Chinese dragons tended to be beneficent creatures, responsible for controlling the weather and so for providing rain in the proper seasons. They resembled the Naga kings of India in their most benevolent mood, and there are so many points of similarity between the two that modern scholars consider that the dragon kings of Chinese mythology are derived from the Naga kings.

Whole books could be compiled on the natural history of dragons from Chinese sources. The differences between male and female dragons are described in detail. Young dragons hatch from eggs, which are usually laid on hillsides near running water, though some of the eggs have an incubation period of hundreds of years. When first hatched the young dragons resemble small lizards, a characteristic which may remind us of the Mordiford dragon (**100**), the Wherwell cockatrice (**28**), and the Lambton

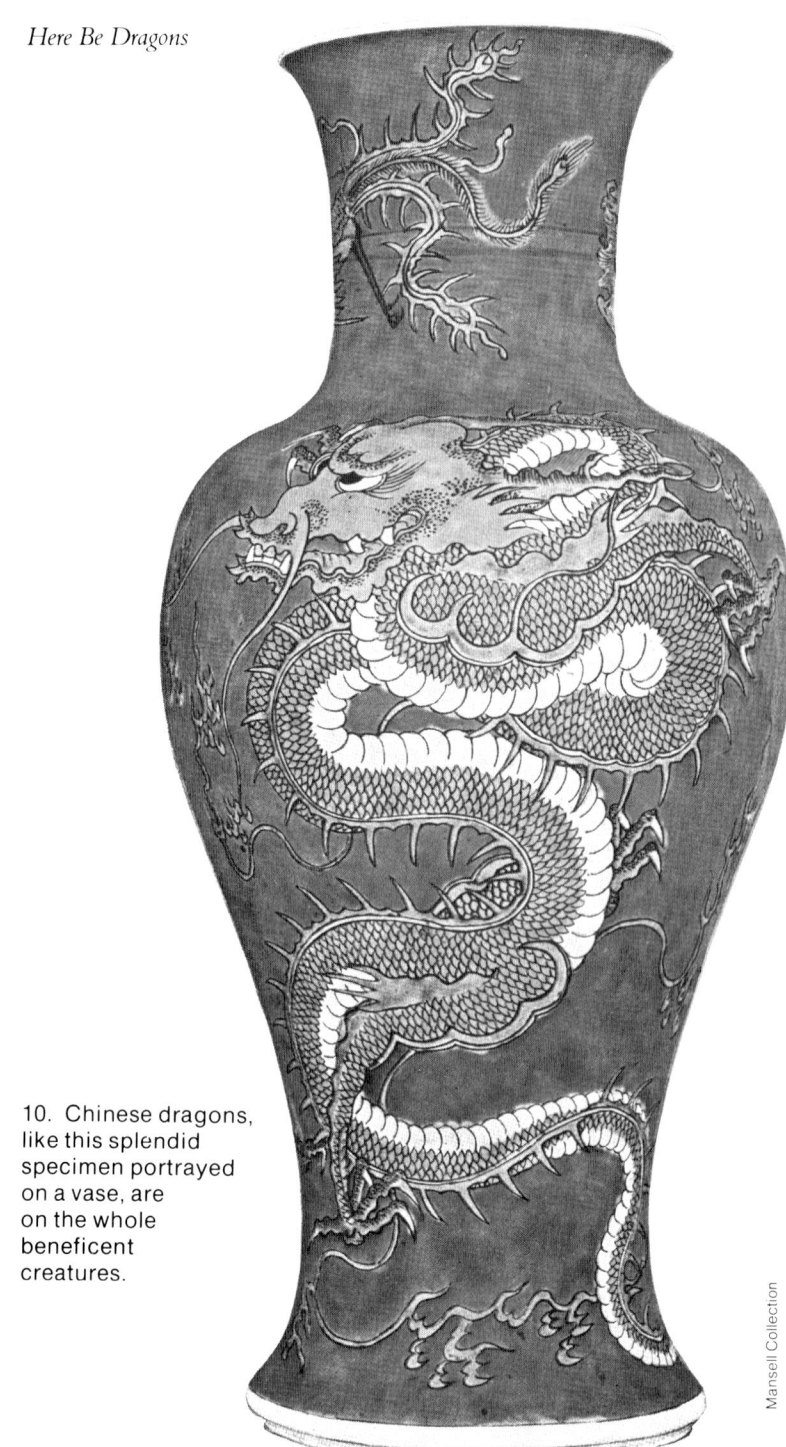

10. Chinese dragons,
like this splendid
specimen portrayed
on a vase, are
on the whole
beneficent
creatures.

worm (**168**), but they grow quickly. The Chinese listed five metamorphoses, with five hundred or a thousand years for each.

Dragons came in many colours, the yellow ones being the most exalted. Experts argued about the number of scales on their bodies, one school of thought maintaining that there were 81 (nine times nine) while another declared that the true number was 117 (nine times nine plus six times six, both nine and six being numbers with important symbolic significance).

Dragons lived such long lives that for practical purposes they could be considered immortal. Yet their bones, skin, teeth, fat, liver, brain, blood and saliva were all of very great value as medicines. The problem of how to obtain these prizes without killing the dragons – a hazardous and unpopular enterprise, for it must be remembered that dragons were also the valued suppliers of rain – was solved by the argument that dragons shed all their organs periodically without damage to themselves, like a snake sloughing its skin. One early emperor, however, the Emperor Chao of the Han dynasty, ate a white dragon he caught in a river and pronounced its flesh very tasty.

The close observation of the behaviour of dragons was recommended to Chinese farmers, who would find this very helpful in forecasting the weather. Dragons leaving their holes to look for water betokened drought; dragons fighting in the air might be a sign of coming rain. Such portents could also foretell human fortunes and were regarded as valuable omens. When we remember, though, that dragons could change their form at will, appearing as such familiar creatures as swallows, crows, spiders and dragonflies, we may recognise Chinese dragon lore as natural history lore in disguise.

Certainly the dragons of China were not the fierce, bloodthirsty monsters of western mythology.

The Near East
In the religious lore of one of the earliest civilisations of the Near East, the Hittites of Asia Minor, a dragon plays a leading part. His name is Illuyankas, and he has earned the displeasure of the weather god, regarded by the Hittites as the King of Heaven, in some way, though whether the god showed it by withholding rain or sending too much is not recorded. The gods encompass his destruction by inviting him and his children to a banquet. There they are given so much food and drink that when the time comes to go home they are too bloated to enter the holes that lead to their den. The gods tie them up and the weather god arrives and kills them all.

As students of the Old Testament are well aware, the god of the Canaanites, the people who occupied the coasts of what are now Palestine and the Lebanon, was Baal. Baal, or Bel, was also a synonym of Marduk, the supreme god of the Babylonian pantheon; the Canaanite Baal, like his Babylonian counterpart, also engaged in a single combat with a dragon-like monster, which he slew. The dragon is named Lotan and is referred to as 'the crooked serpent', 'the primeval serpent', and 'the close-coiling one of seven heads'.

We are led naturally to the Old Testament itself, which is the common heritage of Jews and Christians.

The Old Testament

More than half the references to dragons in the Old Testament can be dismissed as irrelevant to this study, the word translated as 'dragons' in the Authorised Version being *tannim*, which modern authorities say means 'jackals'.

Of the others, some are merely passing references, as in 'Praise the Lord, ye dragons and all deeps' and 'the young lion and dragon shalt thou trample underfoot'. The prophet Jeremiah laments that King Nebuchadnezzar has 'swallowed me up like a dragon'. Isaiah, calling upon the Lord to save his people, makes a cryptic reference to 'it that hath cut Rahab and wounded the Dragon'. He is evidently referring to some folk tale that would be known to his readers.

More specific is his promise that 'in that day with his sore and great and strong sword shall punish Leviathan the piercing serpent, even Leviathan the crooked serpent; and he shall slay the dragon that is in the sea'. The name 'Leviathan' resembles that of Lotan, the dragon slain by Baal; 'the dragon that is in the sea' is evidently a sea-serpent but the prophet may have had the Babylonian myth of Tiamat in mind.

References to Leviathan also occur in two of the Psalms (74 and 104) and in the Book of Job. The writer of the latter book devotes a chapter of thirty-four verses (Chapter 41) to a description of Leviathan, which is obviously some water monster, perhaps a crocodile or even a whale exaggerated by an observer with a vivid imagination. 'Who can open the doors of his face? His teeth are terrible round about. His scales are his pride, shut up together as with a close seal. One is so near to another, that no air can come between them. They are joined one to another, they stick together, that they cannot be sundered...Out of his mouth go burning lamps, and sparks of fire leap out. Out of his nostrils goeth smoke, as out of a seething pot or caldron. His

11. Leviathan, equated in this mediaeval German manuscript with the Antichrist.

breath kindleth coals, and a flame goeth out of his mouth...When he raiseth himself up, the mighty are afraid...The sword of him that layeth at him cannot hold: the spear, the dart, nor the habergeon. He esteemeth iron as straw, and brass as rotten wood... Darts are counted as stubble: he laugheth at the shaking of a spear...He maketh the deep to boil like a pot: he maketh the sea like a pot of ointment. He maketh a path to shine after him; one would think the deep to be hoary. Upon earth there is not his like, who is made without fear.'

Truly a dragon of the noblest vintage!

The Apocrypha

The Apocrypha, which is not now included in the Authorised Version, is the source of a not uncommon feature of dragon stories. This section of Scripture contains a short book with the intriguing title, *The History of the Destruction of Bel and the Dragon*, the hero being Daniel. The scene is set in

39

Babylon, where was 'a great dragon, which they of Babylon worshipped'. Daniel asked permission to 'slay this dragon without sword or staff', and the king, deciding that such a feat was impossible, gave him leave.

'Then Daniel took pitch, and fat, and hair, and did seethe them together, and made lumps thereof; this he put in the dragon's mouth, and so the dragon burst in sunder.'

Daniel's method seems to have been adopted by the Laird of Lariston, who slew the Linton worm (**181**) by dipping a lump of peat in boiling pitch, brimstone and resin and thrusting the titbit down the monster's throat. The Sutherland worm of Cnoc-na-Cnoimh (**190**) was likewise killed by being made to swallow a ball of burning peat dipped in boiling pitch. In two versions of the destruction of the knucker of Lyminster (**32**), the local story-tellers have substituted for this lethal concoction the 'Sussex Pudden', of which Jacqueline Simpson comments that it was 'notoriously heavy and indigestible, especially if eaten cold'. In the story of Billy Biter and the dragon of Filey (**161**) another local dish is employed to bring about the dragon's downfall. The treacle which features largely in its recipe sticks to the dragon's teeth and renders the monster temporarily impotent. In Somerset, where apparently no such dragon-killing delicacy was available, the slayer of the dragon of Kingston St Mary (**12**) had to be content with a boulder, rolled into the dragon's mouth and choking the beast.

The New Testament

The dragon of the *Book of the Revelation of St John the Divine* is the only dragon mentioned in the New Testament. Job's Leviathan (pages 38–9) seems, with due allowance made for poetic exaggeration, to have been an actual living creature. Omitting the flames and sparks, the description could, and perhaps does refer to a crocodile. The great red dragon with seven heads, seen in his vision by St John, is admittedly symbolic imagery. It is, says the seer, identical with 'that old serpent, the Devil, and Satan, which deceiveth the whole world'. The book was born of the atrocious persecution to which Christians were subjected in the early years of the Church and which is reflected in the soaring and horrific word-pictures, piled one on another with such intensity that the reader can find himself sharing the hallucinations of the saint.

Its importance in the study of dragon lore is that the book and its contents were well known throughout western Christendom in the centuries when dragons were apparently most active, and echoes of its thoughts are to be found in many stories of British dragons. Even the relatively mild grampus

of Highclere (**29**) was said to have been banished to the depths of the Red
Sea for a thousand years, just as in the Book of Revelation, 'the dragon, that
old serpent' was bound and cast into a bottomless pit for a thousand years.

Hell fire was an important stock-in-trade of mediaeval Christianity.
One can readily imagine a priest referring his illiterate congregation to a
Doom painting on the church wall, in which the pleasures of the righteous
in paradise are vividly contrasted with the torments of the wicked in hell – a
fiery place, well populated with devils and dragons.

Greek mythology

A study of the dragons of ancient Greece is complicated by their extreme
fecundity. It starts simply enough, with Gaea, the mother of the gods, who
can be identified with Mother Earth. Unfortunately, having a promiscuous
nature, she mated with not only Uranus, the father of the gods, but also
with Tartarus, the god or personification of the Underworld, by whom she
had two children, Echidna and Typhon, both of them monsters.

Typhon is depicted as having numerous dragons heads and wings and
lower parts which are enormous serpents. He is the embodiment of storms
and whirlwinds (hence the word 'typhoon'). After causing much
destruction he is challenged by Zeus, the weather god, who fights him with
lightnings and thunderbolts and eventually chases him down to the
Underworld, throwing Mount Etna on top of him to keep him there
securely. The similarity with the Babylonian and Egyptian myths (pages 34
and 39) is obvious.

The imprisonment of Typhon is not the end of the matter, however.
Before his overthrow Typhon incestuously mated with his sister, Echidna,
who produced a numerous brood of monsters. Among them were the
hydra, the chimaera, the sphinx, Cerberus (the many-headed and dragon-
like dog who guards the Underworld) and many others. Of possibly
different lineage was Pytho, or Delphyne, a tremendous dragon sent by
Hera, wife of Zeus, to deal with Leto, a mistress of Zeus of whom Hera
thoroughly disapproved. This monster was slain by Apollo, Leto's son, a
few minutes after his birth.

The fight between Hercules (or Herakles, in Greek) and the hydra was
the subject of one of the most popular of Greek folk tales. As fast as
Hercules, who was another bastard son of Zeus, struck off one of the
hydra's hundred heads, two or three more grew to take its place. The
problem was eventually solved by setting fire to a neighbouring forest, so
that Hercules was able to cauterise the neck-stumps as each head was struck

12. A French engraving of Hercules dealing with the Hydra by cauterising its neck-stumps.

off, thus preventing any regeneration. With their miraculous ability to heal their wounds immediately, the Crowcombe worm (**11**), the Lambton worm (**168**) and the dragon of Loschy Hill (**155**) are all strongly reminiscent of the hydra.

In the Garden of the Hesperides, Hercules dealt successfully with another dragon with a hundred heads. When visiting the city of Troy he slew a huge sea monster, to whom the king's daughter, Hesione, was about to be sacrificed. In doing battle with the Trojan dragon Hercules allowed himself to be swallowed by it, attacking it from the inside for three days before it expired. Assipattle employed exactly the same tactics in dealing with the Stoor Worm (**191**).

Perseus, yet another son of the god Zeus, was summoned by the king of Ethiopia to rid his kingdom of a sea monster. He arrived just in time to save the king's daughter, Andromeda, who had been chained to a rock in the sea to await the dragon who proposed to have her for his next meal. Perseus duly despatched the creature and married the princess. This exploit provides the basis for the recurrent story of a maiden about to be sacrificed to a dragon and rescued in the nick of time by a hero who kills the dragon

13. Here, the dragon in the Garden of the Hesperides has only one head, but it is commonly portrayed as many-headed.

and is rewarded either by property or by marriage to the heiress he has saved – see page 62. Evidently many a noble family or its ecclesiastical secretaries adopted and adapted a classical legend to support its claim to property: simple country folk were not the only ones to re-shape classical stories to their liking!

Other Greek heroes were also celebrated dragon-killers. There was Cadmus, who prepared the way for the founding of the city of Thebes by killing a dragon which was guarding the only spring in the neighbourhood. Jason, on his quest for the Golden Fleece, found the treasure guarded by a dragon which never slept and which promptly swallowed him, though he was afterwards magically restored to life. To both stories there is a sequel. After the dragon was slain the hero sowed its teeth in furrows, and from them sprang ranks of armed men. Hence the saying, 'sowing dragons' teeth'.

Dragons were sometimes tamed by members of the Greek pantheon. Ceres, the goddess of harvest, possessed a chariot drawn by two winged dragons. A similar chariot with two dragons as steeds bore Medea, the witch who helped Jason steal the Golden Fleece, to flee through the air to

Athens. And one should not forget the various hybrids, such as the Nereids (which were half-women, half-serpent), resulting from the mating of gods (or humans) and dragons.

One of the Greek heroes, Achilles, was invulnerable save for his heel, by which his mother held him when she dipped him in the river Styx. Similarly, certain dragons were vulnerable to blows which landed on only one small spot. In the Castle Carlton dragon (**123**) the spot was a wart on its right thigh; in the Wantley dragon (**158**) it was the middle of its back; in the Newcastle Emlyn wyvern (**109**) it was, remarkably for a dragon, its navel!

Alexander the Great was reputed in mediaeval romances to have been borne aloft in what appears to have been something resembling the basket of an air balloon, the motive power for which was supplied by two griffins. In pictures of Alexander's flight into the heavens they are usually shown tethered on either side of the basket, in true heraldic postures. A lump of meat on a spear above the basket is the bait which persuades them to soar.

Prehistoric Europe

The ram, the bull, the horse, the reindeer and the other animals, representing probably local gods, may have been well established in Britain several thousand years before the dragon. There is some confusion over just what animal or creature certain effigies are supposed to portray, but the Padstow and Minehead osses (**1** and **23**), the Antrobus horn dancers (**141**) and the Hooden Horse (**37**), as well as the Old Tup of the North Midlands, the Mari Lwyd of South Wales and other characters in regional folk drama, seem to have their origins far back in prehistory. There may well be a direct link between them and the palaeolithic cave paintings of southern Europe, which depict men with animal horns and masks engaging in some sort of ritual. By comparison Snap, the Norwich dragon (**85**), may be a late-comer, introduced with the St George cult in the early Middle Ages and representing the blurred distinction between hobby horses, dragons and other winged or horned creatures.

A surprising number of dragon and serpent stories are associated with acknowledged prehistoric sites. The dragons of the Exe Valley (**5**) have their homes in two Iron Age hill forts. The Manaton dragon (**6**) haunted an old Dartmoor tin-mine, with Bronze Age relics all around. The Challacombe dragons (**7**) likewise lived in a group of Bronze Age barrows on Exmoor. The Norton Fitzwarren dragon (**13**) belonged to an Iron Age hill fort near Taunton and was associated with a great battle once fought there. Cissbury Hill, in Sussex, which is crowned by a prehistoric earthwork, is said to be haunted by 'monstrous serpents' (**34**). The White Horse of Uffington, in Berkshire (**46**), has in a key position its Dragon's Hill. Dragons are said to guard buried treasure in tumuli near Bilsdale (Yorkshire – **163**), Garsington (Oxfordshire – **64**), Drakelowe (Derbyshire – **130**), Gunnarton Fell (Northumberland – **180**), and no doubt others as well. Some students of folklore profess to see great spiral, processional ways winding around certain sacred hills, notably Glastonbury Tor.

Rome

The Romans, being less imaginative than the Greeks, took over most of the Greek myths and folk stories, changing the names of the heroes, gods and villains but making few other alterations. It was left to Pliny, sometimes termed the father of natural history, to record a marvellous piece of dragon lore. He asserts that in Ethiopia several dragons will, in times of scarcity, weave and interlace themselves together to form a lattice resembling an osier hurdle. Then, holding their heads erect, they launch themselves on the sea off the coast of East Africa and so sail to India, in the hopes of better pickings.

14. Are the terraces winding around Glastonbury Tor, a sacred hill of antiquity, the remains of processional pathways?

Aerofilms

15. Standards of the Roman army, including two recognisable as dragons.

The dragon was officially adopted by the Roman army as one of its emblems. Just as the eagle was the standard of a legion, so the dragon was the standard of a cohort, which was a unit of approximately five hundred men. Apparently the dragon standard was not so much a banner bearing a dragon device as a three-dimensional fabrication like a windsock, and it has been suggested that it served the subsidiary purpose of helping the archers to gauge wind strength and direction. Ingenious soldiers sometimes fixed to

46

their dragons devices which hissed or whistled when held aloft in a breeze, while at the same time their long tails lashed about realistically.

The Romans adopted dragon banners from their traditional eastern enemies, the Parthians and the Persians, who seem to have derived them from central Asia. The device was apparently well known to the various semi-nomads of central Asia who, at intervals throughout history, have brought havoc and ruin to the settled lands around them. In the Middle Ages further refinements were added; dragon banners, flown as kites, were equipped with lighted torches so that they belched out flames and smoke as they soared and dipped overhead, and as late as the thirteenth century the Tartars swept deep into central Europe and won a battle against the Polish army largely through the employment of fire-emitting, smoke-producing dragon banners, which the Poles took to be supernatural allies of the invaders.

While in due course familiarity transferred these fearsome apparitions to the realm of heraldry and legend, the effect on the mind of an illiterate soldier seeing them for the first time and totally unprepared for the sight must have been traumatic. Lucian, the Roman satirist, writing towards the end of the second century AD, described the reactions of such a soldier of Rome who was convinced that the creatures were alive: 'He said they were alive and of enormous size; that they were born in Persia, a little way beyond Iberia; that they are bound to long poles and, raised on high, create terror while the Parthians are coming on from a distance; that in the encounter itself at close quarters they are freed and sent against the enemy; that in fact they had swallowed many of our men and coiled themselves around others and suffocated and crushed them.'

Long before the Roman legions left Britain, however, Roman soldiers were thoroughly familiar with aerial dragons and were using them for their own purposes. It must not be supposed that all memory of them died immediately the armies departed. On the contrary, Celts of the post-Roman era adopted the dragon as their emblem, as is evident not only from the name and reputed associations of Uther Pendragon, of the immediate post-Roman period, but also from the fact that a red dragon is the emblem of Wales today: the Welsh, who were in part descendants of the Romano-British of the days of the Empire, and the Anglo-Saxons, who had a long history as mercenaries in the Roman armies, both derived their dragon standards from Rome. If we were able to interview the 'aged inhabitant of Penllin' who in about 1900 described the scintillating winged dragons he said he had seen in his boyhood days (**105**) we would doubtless have found him admitting that he himself had not seen them; it was his father who had told him about them. In fact, he testified that his father and uncle had killed some of them, because they were 'as bad as foxes for poultry'. If we could have questioned the father and uncle in their turn, no doubt they would have added a few details but would have mentioned that it was not they but their father who had actually encountered the dragons. And so, by gentle stages, the long chain of human memory would have taken us back through the centuries to the days when the Roman dragon standards flew over Wales. Human memory, especially when uncluttered by the written word and by the modern distractions of radio and television, is quite capable of such feats.

America

Dragons are not confined to the Old World. Apart from pictures of dragons gratuitously scattered over maps of America by early European cartographers, dragons featured in the folklore and mythology of various Indian peoples, while in a National Park in Adams County, Ohio, is the huge effigy of a serpent, constructed by heaping up continuous mounds of earth. More than 400 yards long, it is situated on a cliff-top in wooded country. The body is sinuous or serpentine, the tail tightly coiled, and the head raised with jaws agape. Within the jaws is an ovoid object which could be intended to represent an egg. Known as the Great Serpent Mound,

Dr Georg Gerster/John Hillelson Agency

16. This huge effigy of a serpent, consisting of continuous mounds of earth, is in the National Park in Adams County, Ohio.

this strange figure has so far defied attempts by archaeologists to date or explain it.

In the highly complex Mayan pantheon, Itzamna, the son of the supreme god Hunab Ku, is depicted as an old, cross-eyed, bearded man with the body of a lizard or dragon. Itzamna is the god of the heavens and of day and night and the instructor of mankind in the arts of writing, medicine, the cultivation of food plants and other important subjects.

As in the mythologies of the Old World, there are on a lower plane a host of monstrous creatures. The Chorti, one branch of the Maya people, testify to the existence of four Chiccans, which are gigantic serpents, each living in a large lake. In addition, innumerable minor Chiccans live in streams, lakes and springs, migrating to the hills in the dry season when the lowland waters dry up. These Chiccans are responsible for causing floods, earthquakes and storms.

Quetzalcoatl, one of the chief gods of the Aztecs, who later, through conquest, was absorbed into the Mayan pantheon and was known as Kukulcan, had as his sign the feathered serpent, which nearly resembled some of the winged dragons of contemporary Europe.

The North

Our ancestors were familiar with dragons before ever they heard of St George and before dragons became a favourite theme of mediaeval church-builders. Back in the ninth and tenth centuries, men shuddered with dread at the sight of the dragon figureheads carved on the prows of pirate Viking ships, the invaders from the North.

Dragons feature in the mythology of the North as in that of warmer southern lands but in somewhat different roles. No dragon is involved in the primary acts of Creation nor in the ancestry of gods or humans. The great Northern dragon is Nidhoggr, the dread biter, who lurks in the Underworld, gnawing steadily at the roots of Yggdrasil, the huge ash tree which supports the universe. When it succeeds, even temporarily, the end of the world will come. Its efforts are, however, thwarted by a race of supernatural beings called Norns, who restore the Tree every day by watering it from a magic well.

The pantheon of Norse gods includes an enigmatic character named Loki, who, like Lucifer in Hebrew myths and Seth in the celestial hierarchy of ancient Egypt, was once a benevolent and reliable god but later fell from grace and became a hostile entity. In his latter, terrible metamorphosis Loki became the parent of a brood of monsters, among which were the Serpent

49

Archiv für Kunst und Geschichte

17. A nineteenth-century depiction of the slaying of the dragon Fafnir by the hero Sigurd, or Siegfried.

of Midgard (meaning the populated Earth), the ravening wolf Fenrir, and a female monster named Hel who inherited, as a goddess, the realm of the Underworld.

By the efforts of the benevolent gods, particularly Thor, all were put under restraint. With Hel safely in the Underworld, Fenrir is bound with fetters and the Serpent of Midgard is banished to the depths of the sea, where it becomes the great sea-serpent described in the Orcadian myth as the Stoor Worm (**191**). But the time will come when all three monsters will be released and will return to plague the world of men. An Ice Age will develop, winter following winter with no intervening summers. There will be earthquakes, volcanoes, tidal waves and clouds of toxic gases. The gods will emerge to do battle with the evil forces but will fail. So doomed humanity will plunge to extinction, save for one man and one woman who, in due course, will start the cycle all over again. The entire concept bears some startling resemblances to the Apocalypse as described in the last book of the Bible, and early Norse converts to Christianity were able to find much common ground in certain elements of their old religion.

In addition to this cosmic vision, Northern mythology, like that of Greece, contains a number of stories of human heroes who challenged and slew dragons. One was Beowulf who, as recounted in the epic poem of the seventh or eighth century AD, killed his dragon but died soon after his victory through the monster's poison. Another was Sigurd, or Siegfried, whose destruction of the dragon Fafnir is immortalised by Wagner's opera-cycle, *The Ring*. There was also Hromind Greipson, who descended into a cave to fight with and slay the dragon-king, Thrain.

Echoes of Norse mythology are naturally strongest in the Orkneys and Shetland. The Norse brood of sea-monsters is represented not only by the legend of the Stoor Worm (**191**) but by the njuggles of Shetland (**193**) and the Nuckelavee of Orkney (**192**), as well as by the nøkk of Norway.

Post-Roman Europe

The Romano-British inhabitants of Britain were plagued by another race of savage marauders with a similar folklore, the Anglo-Saxons. The knucker of Lyminster, in Sussex (**32**), derives its name from the Anglo-Saxon *nicor*, a water monster. The Anglo-Saxons, it seems, used dragons as emblems on their war banners: we read of the golden dragon of Mercia and the wyvern of Wessex. The story of the battle between the red dragon of Wales and the white dragon of the Saxons, which beasts the magician Merlin found sleeping in the waters of a hidden lake beneath Mount

Snowdon, evidently dates from this period. So probably does the account of the fight between a black dragon and a spotted red dragon on the banks of the river Stour, where it forms the border between Essex and Suffolk (**79**), in spite of the fact that the date is given as 1449.

His very name qualified Uther Pendragon, father of King Arthur, to be an associate of dragons. One version of his knightly emblem was a dragon which occupied virtually the whole of the shield, while other mediaeval authorities asserted that his arms should probably be two green dragons back to back. Geoffrey of Monmouth, that twelfth-century purveyor of tall tales, declared that instead of a horse, Uther Pendragon had a golden dragon to carry him to the wars.

King Arthur himself is said to have fought with at least one dragon, but the contest took place not in Britain but at a village in Brittany. Sir Lancelot also had a reputation as a dragon-killer. St Simon Stylites, who lived for years on the top of a pillar, was once responsible for taming a dragon which had its den near the spot where the saint was practising his self-mortification. One day the dragon went blind through getting a splinter (or stake) in its eye, whereupon the saint cured it.

In the Bayeux Tapestry a dragon is depicted flying over the head of Harold, the English king, at the Battle of Hastings (see also page 17).

Dragons were as common in mediaeval Europe as in England, and for most countries a book such as this, with at least an equal number of entries, could be compiled. Mention can be made of only a few of them, one of the most striking being undoubtedly the Tarasque.

This dragon, which was said to be larger than an ox, with six legs, spiky scales and a serpent's tail, was a water monster who lived near the confluence of the rivers Rhone and Durance, not far from the little town of Tarascon. It was the offspring of Leviathan and a particularly foul creature called a Bonnacon which, when pursued, defecated, causing trees and other objects splashed by its faeces to burst into flames. The Tarasque was already in existence when Hercules visited the district and defeated the king, Tauriscus, in a battle there. The Tarasque survived the attentions of that celebrated dragon-killer, however, but eventually fell to a female saint – St Martha according to some versions, St Margaret in others – who so tamed it that she was able to lead it docilely into the town, her girdle around its neck. Effigies of the Tarasque are still paraded around the town on Ascension Day. The chief one is larger than the Norwich Snap (**85**) or any of the English hobby horses, requiring three men to carry it, and its head and tail both move about. Its general appearance and construction, however, are much the same, and its parade through the streets is accompanied by much boisterous horse play.

A famous dragon which lived in Rhodes was slain by Deodatus de Gozano, a celebrated knight of the Order of St John, in a classic battle in which the more heroic part was played by two of his dogs, which he had specially trained for the purpose. One version of this epic, however, states that the dragon was killed by the expedient of inducing it to consume large quantities of quicklime and then allowing it to drink copiously.

THE NATURAL HISTORY OF DRAGONS

No one has yet been able to take an indisputable photograph of a real live dragon or similar monster anywhere, apart from the Komodo Dragons (see page 53). The fact that so many dragons became extinct before the age of photography does not help, of course. How splendid it would be to have coloured photographs of the scintillating dragons of Penllin Castle, Glamorgan (**105**), which an old man who died about the year 1900 asserted he saw as a boy and described as very beautiful: 'They looked as if they were covered with jewels of all sorts. Some of them had crests sparkling with all the colours of the rainbow.' When disturbed they flew out of their dens 'sparkling all over', as they glided 'over people's heads, with outspread wings bright, and sometimes with eyes, too, like the feathers in a peacock's tail'. This was the old man who testified that his father and uncle used to kill some of them, because they were 'as bad as foxes for the poultry'.

Wouldn't they have been grand television subjects!

As it is, we have to make do with artists' impressions, which in the case of the Loch Ness monster were made by eye-witnesses, in one instance by Sir Peter Scott. Farther back in history the evidence is supplied by paintings, stained glass windows and carvings in stone and wood in churches. Details of many of these sculptures are found in the Gazetteer (pages 71–157).

Species of dragons
There are, of course, several species of dragons, as there are of elephants and vultures. Some have four legs, some two and some apparently none at all. Many dragons can fly, though some are wingless, and the wings of some of the others seem hardly large enough to support the heavy bodies. They are of all colours, those which used to infest the fields of South Wales being

53

18. The Wherwell cockatrice (**28**) shows the physical characteristics of a wyvern as well as the deadly cockatrice's eye. It exhausted itself by fighting its own reflection in a polished steel mirror.

particularly scintillating. Species of which only one or two examples are known will be dealt with in the Gazetteer as they occur.

Cockatrices. The chief characteristic of these creatures was that they had such a baleful eye that a direct look could kill. An early collector of monster stories, Edward Topsell, writing in 1608, states, though he says he cannot help laughing about the tales, 'I have often heard it confidently related that once our nation was full of cockatrices, and that a certain man did destroy them by going up and down in glasse, whereby their own shapes were reflected upon their own faces, and so they died.'

Wyverns. These were two-legged dragons with bat-like wings and arrow-tipped tails. They are closely associated with Wales and the West Country, but a mediaeval armorial portrays two wyverns, wingless and with necks and tails intertwined, as the arms of, of all unlikely persons, the King of Barbary.

Griffins. Only dragons with the heads of eagles qualify as griffins.

Dragon behaviour and appearance
Dragons in general seem to be harmless when young, and content with a

54

milk diet. As they grow older they become carnivorous and end up by becoming man-eaters (though Chinese dragons are exceptional in being, on the whole, benevolent creatures). When the Mordiford dragon (**100**) was a small green creature, 'no bigger than a cucumber', it was the pet of a little girl named Maud, and see what it became later (though admittedly it never turned against Maud). Similarly, the Wherwell cockatrice (**28**) and the Lambton worm (**168**) were both considered harmless at the start of their terrible careers.

There are just a few exceptions to the general dragon characteristics of hell-raising, destruction and devouring stray humans. The outstanding one is the dragon of Carhampton, Somerset (**16**), which, according to a sixteenth-century translation of a mediaeval document, was 'a huge and terrible serpent which had devastated many fields'. St Carantoc, having been asked to rid the district of this monster, went and prayed about the matter, whereupon 'the serpent came to him straight away with a great roar, like a calf running to its mother, and bowed its head before the servant of God like a slave obedient to its master, humble and gentle-eyed. And he put a stole round its neck and led it away like a lamb. Its neck was like a bull's neck, and the stole would hardly go round it.' One would think this was an eye-witness account, so graphic are the details! Predictably, the people who saw the dragon thus subdued wanted to kill it, but St Carantoc, a man of the quality of St Francis of Assissi, would not allow it. He made the dragon promise it would never again harm anyone but would go far away, and then released it.

Another exceptional dragon was that of Castle Gwys or Wiston, in Pembrokeshire (**110**). This cockatrice could be said hardly to have had an existence of its own but was simply a device for testing claimants to the Wiston estates. The successful claimant had to prove that he had seen the dragon without himself being seen, a feat eventually accomplished by an ingenious fellow who allowed himself to be rolled in a barrel to the cockatrice's lair, where he spied it through the bung-hole.

Apart from these two and a few other eccentric specimens, dragons in general followed a conventional pattern of behaviour, committing an increasing tally of atrocities. Some dragons show a partiality for succulent young maidens for dinner. Dragons are protected by an armour-coating of scales and are armed with sharp teeth and fiery breath. The Saffron Walden cockatrice (**42**) 'blasteth all Plants with his breath, it burneth everything it goeth over; no herb can grow near his place of abode.' As with others of its tribe, this cockatrice can kill with a look. 'If a man touch it though with a long pole it kills him; and if it sees a man afar off it destroys him with its looks.'

Other dragons kill their victim by coiling their serpent-like bodies around it and squeezing, like a boa constrictor. Yet others possess a poisonous sting. The monstrous Linton worm (**181**) had such powerful lungs that it simply took a deep breath and sucked in any sheep or cattle that happened to be nearby.

Eye-witness accounts of dragons provide interesting details. The Longwitton dragon (**179**) had a long black tongue and lapped water like a dog. It also had a long, lizard-like tail and a warty skin. The wyvern of Cynwch Lake (**143**) moved with a kind of arching movement, like a looper caterpillar, and left a slimy, slug-like trail. The remarkable Penllin serpents (**105**) looked 'as if they were covered with jewels of all colours'.

Although dragons apparently hatch from eggs and are quite small at birth, incongruously the Newcastle Emlyn wyvern (**109**) boasted a navel. Some female dragons have a strong maternal instinct, as is illustrated by one version of the story of the dragon of Ben Vair (**185**), who battered herself to death against a seaside rock on realising that her dragonets had been burnt to death.

Physical explanations?

The word 'dragon' comes from the Latin *draco*, which was in turn derived from the Greek *drakon*, meaning a serpent. And in the records the words 'dragon', 'worm' and 'serpent' are often used indiscriminately, to describe the same creature. Are we perhaps in some instances dealing with real serpents?

Certainly in some of the later episodes we are. The 'very great and monstrous serpent', sixteen feet long, which 'a certain Italian brought into the cittie of Durham' on 11 June 1568, can be written down as a snake (**171**). Statements that it had a girth 'greater than a great horse' and that, before coming to England, it had 'devoured more than a 1000 persons and destroyed a whole countrey' can be discounted.

The dragon or serpent seen in St Leonards Forest, Sussex (**33**), in August 1614 also sounds like a real snake, perhaps a large cobra. The 'two great bunches so big as a large foote-ball upon either side of him' could be a cobra's opened hood, though some of the observers who reported it thought they were rudimentary wings. It had a blackish back, red underparts, was thickest 'in the middest', tapering at both ends and was estimated to be about nine feet long. 'He is of countenance very proud and at the sight or hearing of men or cattel will raise his neck upright and seem to listen and looke about, with great arrogancy.' Beyond much doubt an exotic snake, probably escaped from some menagerie.

Some of the more antique dragons also possessed snake-like characteristics, notably a lack of legs, a habit of killing their victims by coiling around them and squeezing and another habit of coiling their body in a spiral when at rest. The Crowcombe worm (**11**) had a body thicker than the trunks of three oak trees but apparently no legs. The knucker of Lyminster (**32**) was said to have been a water serpent, as was the Brinsop dragon of Herefordshire (**101**). The dragon of Loschy Hill (**155**) attempted to kill Sir Peter Loschy by winding its coils around him and constricting its body. The Lambton worm (**168**) used the same tactics. The Linton worm (**181**) would coil itself around a hill when sunning itself after a meal, creating a series of spiralling terraces, a custom also followed by the serpent of Dalry (**183**). The worm of Cnoc-na-Cnoimh (**190**) similarly wrapped itself around its native hill in its death struggles.

It seems certain that the monster killed by the people of Wormingford or Bures, on the Essex/Suffolk border, in or about the year 1405 was a crocodile (**79**). Indeed, there is a local folk memory that it was a 'cockadrille' brought back from the Near East by the crusading King Richard I and housed for a time in his menagerie in the Tower of London, from whence it escaped. This seems reasonable enough, but understandably the creature was also put on records as a dragon, and a stained glass window in Wormingford church portraying St George killing the dragon was probably inspired by it.

Possibly there were other individual snakes or crocodiles at the source of other myths. The Solway sea-worm (**182**) may well have been a real sea creature, perhaps a whale, stranded on a beach. And there are more recent reports of sea monsters off Shetland. Should we seek dragon origins in them?

The literature of sea monsters is voluminous, and there can be no denying that there is plenty of room in the oceans for them to exist. In France, at a *Centre de Cryptozoologie* in the Dordogne, Dr Bernard Heuvelmans, who has written several books on the unknown animals of the world, finds that many of the mysteries reported to him concern sea creatures.

One recent sighting of an unknown monster was made by John Ridgway and Chay Blyth when rowing across the Atlantic in 1966. Ridgway records that when at the oars on a quiet, tranquil night he suddenly became aware of 'a swishing noise to starboard. I looked out over the water and suddenly

19. An artist's impression of a sea serpent seen by the frigate HMS *Daedalus* between the Cape of Good Hope and St Helena on 6 August 1848.

Ann Ronan Picture Library

saw the writhing, twisting shape of a great creature…It was an enormous size, some 35 or more feet, and it came towards me quite fast…It headed straight at me and disappeared right beneath me…I reluctantly had to believe that there was only one thing it could have been – a sea-serpent.'

During the war J. D. Starkey, aboard an Admiralty trawler in the Indian Ocean, was keeping watch one night when he observed a giant squid lying alongside. He could clearly see that it was at least the length of the ship, which was more than 175 feet long.

Off the island of Soay, in the Outer Hebrides, in 1959 two Scotsmen, out mackerel fishing, encountered a sea monster which they declared was 'definitely reptilian'. The head was about 2½ feet high, with big, protruding eyes, and they saw about 8 or 10 feet of the creature's back above water.

When in 1915 the British ship *Iberian* was torpedoed in the North Atlantic it exploded underwater a few seconds after sinking. 'A little later pieces of wreckage, and among them a gigantic sea animal, writhing and struggling wildly, were shot out of the water to a height of 60 to 100 feet...It was about 60 feet long, was like a crocodile in shape and had four limbs with powerful webbed feet and a long tail tapering to a point.' The phenomenon was seen by at least four or five reliable observers.

Heuvelmans, having carefully studied the reported sightings of sea monsters and having eliminated hoaxes and obviously invertebrate creatures such as squids and octopuses, claims to have been able to identify nine different types. Some seem to be mammals, others reptilian. Are there any which might be identifiable as prehistoric and supposedly extinct reptiles, such as the plesiosaur?

The question is doubly relevant because it has been suggested that the Loch Ness monster (**187**) might be a plesiosaur. Indeed, after studying the computer treatment of a series of fuzzy underwater pictures of 'Nessie', taken by an expedition from the Academy of Applied Science of Boston, Massachusetts, in 1975, Sir Peter Scott has painted a reconstruction of the creatures portrayed, and plesiosaurs they almost certainly are by this interpretation. Scientists are less sceptical about the survival of creatures from distant geological times since the discovery in 1952 of the coelacanth, a fish that was supposed to have become extinct about 300 million years ago.

Jacqueline Simpson, while admitting that if plesiosaurs do survive they could easily account for the alleged monsters of the Scottish lochs and of lakes in many other countries, raises the objection that the Loch Ness species has been 'remarkably discreet about its funerals. For 60 million years it has contrived to dispose of its dead so neatly that not a bone, not a claw, not a scale or a tooth has ever been brought to light.'

Fair comment, and if substantiated it would eliminate plesiosaurs. F. W. Holiday proposes as an alternative a huge worm-like creature that feeds on sediment. He points out that the 1970 survey of Loch Morar (**188**) showed that the ooze at the bottom of the lake contains about 25% organic matter. A worm-like monster, which perhaps 'might forage over the bottom like a catfish and make troughs or channels in the mud', would find plenty of food. It so happens that a fossil of a creature approximating to that description was discovered in coal deposits near Chicago in 1966. Given the name of *Tulli monstrum gregarium*, it was a 'worm-like creature with a tiny head and long, flexible neck and a long, torpedo-shaped body ending in a powerful tail'.

If prehistoric creatures have survived in deep lakes and in the oceans, could the same be true of land monsters? In particular, are there still examples of the dinosaurs, which are supposed to have become extinct sixty million or so years ago, still living in the world? There are those who believe that there are. Quite recently expeditions have been in central Africa searching for monster reptiles of which they have heard reports. Again, there are plenty of suitable and unexplored habitats in the forests and swamps of Africa and South America.

If there *are* such creatures alive today in remote and inaccessible corners of the world, possibly a few thousand years ago some of them were surviving in, say, the Nile or the Euphrates or the forests of the north. There need not have been many. Just one, who happened to achieve the correct associations in religion or folklore, would have been enough. Human memory is capable of astonishing feats.

One example from recent times will serve to demonstrate that not all the mysteries of the world's more remote regions are yet revealed to us and to support the suggestion that traditional features of dragons derive from animals which actually existed. A book entitled *Mythical Monsters*, written in 1886 by Charles Gould, speculated that a real dragon might have existed and described what it was probably like: 'We may infer that it was a long terrestrial lizard, hibernating and carnivorous, with the power of constricting its snake-like body and tail; possibly furnished with wing-like expansions of its integument, after the fashion of *draco volans* and capable of occasional progress on its hind legs alone when excited in attack...Probably it preferred sandy open country to forest land...Although terrestrial, it probably, in common with most reptiles, enjoyed frequent bathing, and when not so engaged, or basking in the sun, secluded itself under some overhanging bank or cavern.'

Yes, that is a fair description of what a dragon might be like, assuming one had existed at a time recent enough for men to have seen it alive. But no one suspected that some had still survived and, when the giant Monitor lizards were discovered on the convict island of Komodo, in what is now Indonesia, in 1912, people at first refused to believe it. The Komodo dragons are now a well-established fact, and they answer Gould's description quite well. Some of them are twelve feet long, and they are indeed carnivorous, though they seldom if ever attack man. Now there are reports of an even larger 'dragon', over twenty feet long, in the jungles of the neighbouring island of New Guinea.

The Komodo dragons lived in seclusion on their remote island for so long that it seems unlikely that anyone from the West ever encountered them before 1912. Certainly the chances against any of them being conveyed to

20. Giant Monitor lizards from the Indonesian island of Komodo – the Komodo dragons.

Ardea London

lands in the West in classical times would seem to be astronomical. But the bare possibility does remain, especially if we concede that the information about the creatures may have come via China.

The world has not yet yielded up all its secrets. There may be other creatures as startling as the Komodo dragon still to be revealed. Infra-red night-scopes, sonar, underwater cameras, aerial surveys and other modern technical equipment may produce some exciting discoveries within the coming decades. Perhaps then we shall have to revise our ideas about the origin of dragons yet again.

61

FIRST CATCH YOUR DRAGON

The dragon-slayers

The typical hero of a dragon legend is someone local, and in almost all instances he is one of two types: either the local lord (or the heir to the local lord), or an ingenious commoner. Of some stories there are alternative versions, one with a hero of one type, and one with a hero of the other. For the slaying of the Mordiford dragon (**100**) there are no fewer than five different versions. For Lyminster (**32**) there are three.

Of the Mordiford stories three present the hero as a criminal under sentence of death, who is reprieved as a reward for killing the dragon. The variations are in the methods he employs. The fourth story gives the credit to the villagers of Mordiford, who crept up and hacked the dragon to death when it was sleeping off the effects of a big meal. In the fifth version, however, the champion is a local lord, a member of the Garston family, who, incidentally, had a wyvern on their crest.

This version introduces an element common to many dragon stories; they are advanced as an explanation of how a family, well known locally, came to acquire their estates. After the slaying of the Castle Carlton dragon (**123**), for instance, the champion, Sir Hugh Bardolfe, is granted extensive lands, exemption from certain tolls, the right to display a dragon on his arms, the privilege of taking 'a horn of salt from every salt cart passing through his domain', and several other rewards. At Moston (Cheshire – **140**) the fortunes of the Venables family, who display a dragon on their crest, are founded on a grant of land made in recognition of the prowess of Sir Thomas Venables, who shot an arrow into the eye of a dragon which was about to swallow a child. The Somervilles of Linton (Roxburghshire – **181**) claimed the title to the lands and lordship of Linton, as well as the office of Royal Falconer to the King of Scotland, by virtue of the deed of an ancestor who rid the countryside of the Linton worm.

In a number of instances the hero receives as part of his reward the hand of a local heiress, sometimes a princess, in marriage. An outstanding example is Assipattle, who slew the Stoor Worm by descending into its stomach and interfering with its internal organs and who married the daughter of the King of Orkney (**191**). Scaw, the hero of the Handale (Yorkshire) story (**159**), was rewarded by marriage with an earl's daughter and, of course, great estates. The same theme occurs in the anomalous story of the Laidly Worm (**178**), in which the dragon is a bewitched princess who needs the ministrations of a handsome hero to restore her to her rightful

Crewe Library

21. Sir Thomas Venables about to despatch the Moston dragon (**140**), which he has just shot in the eye with an arrow, thus rescuing the child which was to have been the dragon's next meal.

form. Naturally he then marries her. One gains the impression, though, that in these stories the estates are the important thing; the girl is a nice little romantic embellishment, but one which goes right back to the stories of Perseus and St George.

At the other end of the social scale, the local peasants who are credited with the destruction of dragons are a mixed lot. In a few instances such a hero is identified simply as 'a local lad' or 'a villager' but in others not only his occupation but his name is specifically stated. Thus the slayer of the Deerhurst (Gloucestershire) dragon (**57**) is John Smith, a labourer; that of the dragon of Cnoc-na-Cnoimh (**190**) a farmer named Hector Gunn; the hero who ingeniously manipulated the dragon of Ben Vair to its doom was Charles the Skipper (**185**). Assipattle, who killed the Stoor Worm in the Orkneys (**191**), was the youngest of seven sons and was reputed to be a dreamer. Into the story of the Filey dragon (**161**) creeps an element of farce, the hero being a hen-pecked tailor, Billy Biter. A blacksmith appears in at least two stories – those of Dalry (**183**) and Llandeilo Graban (**112**) – which is not surprising, for the devices by which the respective dragons were overcome demanded the services of a smith. The killer of the Wherwell cockatrice (**28**) was a man named Green, a servant at the local Priory. The Kellington dragon (**157**) was slain by Ormroyd, a shepherd. Three brothers appear in the role of champions in the curious story of the dragon of Winlatter Rock (**132**). In one version of the tale of the knucker of Lyminster (**32**), the local boy who is responsible for its slaughter is named Jim Puttock; in another, Jim Pulk.

The variations in the tale of the Mordiford dragon (**100**, and see page 62) probably illustrate the development of these stories. There the Garstons, a member of whose family was the original hero, eventually left the district and were forgotten. The story, which had been used to account for their possession of the Mordiford estates, no longer meant anything to the local people. The story, however, was a good one, worth repeating by one generation to the next. So in typical country style, the villagers substituted one of themselves for the long-departed scion of the Garston family. In fact, in this instance they went right to the bottom of the social scale and made the hero a criminal under sentence of death.

Jim Pulk, Jim Puttock, Hector Gunn, Billy Biter, Charlie the Skipper and the rest are homely characters whom the listeners could believe in, which perhaps explains why knights errant, or wandering knights with no local connections, while common enough in mediaeval romances, are much rarer in British dragon stories.

How to kill a dragon

That dragons should have to be killed by a spear thrust down their throat seems reasonable enough, in a view of the formidable scaly armour which covered most of their body. Nor is it surprising that, in the dragon-killing depicted in Shobdon church (**103**), the weapon which Christ is thrusting down the dragon's throat is a cross.

However, dragons are such formidable adversaries that it is legitimate to employ any kind of ruse and stratagem to accomplish their defeat, even some that might be considered unfair. A common device is for the dragon-killer to encase himself in armour not unlike the scales of the dragon, except that the hero's shining scales are sharp blades or spikes, on which the dragon wounds itself as it closes in. Sir Maurice de Berkeley, who slew the Bisterne dragon (**27**), covered his armour with bird-lime and powdered glass. At

Dalry (**183**) the hero was a local blacksmith who had made for himself a suit of armour with retractable spikes, which caused irretrievable havoc in the serpent's inside after the champion had allowed himself to be swallowed. Sir Peter Loschy, when killing the dragon of Loschy Hill (**155**), wore armour covered with razor blades, relying on the observed habit of the dragon of dealing with its victims by wrapping its coils around them and squeezing tight. The heir to the Lambton estates had his armour studded with spikes (**168**). The dragons of Llandeilo Graban (**112**) and Llanrhaeadr (**142**) destroyed themselves by wrapping their bodies around effigies covered with spikes and knives.

At Saffron Walden (**42**) and Horndon (**39**) the dragon-killers relied not on spiked but highly polished armour, that of the 'valerous knight' of Saffron Walden being a 'coat of christall glass'. In both instances the implication is that the dragon succumbed not to the dazzling effect of light on the armour but to the sight of its own reflection. In certain other examples, such as that of the Wherwell cockatrice (**28**), the monster mistakes its reflection for another cockatrice and batters itself to the point of exhaustion in trying to expel the intruder from its den. But there is a suggestion that for a cockatrice, with its lethal eye, to look at itself in a mirror or a polished suit of armour was tantamount to committing suicide.

Another frequent feature of dragon-killing stories is the death of the hero in the moment of victory or shortly afterwards. It occurs in the stories of the Bisterne dragon (**27**), one version of the Aller dragon (**14**), the dragon of Loschy Hill (**155**), the Slingsby dragon (**156**) and several others. At Penmynydd (**144**) it is the heir to the local estate who dies, in fulfilment of a prophecy. At La Hogue Bie, in Jersey (**31**), the hero is evilly slain when resting, exhausted, after his battle. At Lambton (**168**) the victim is the champion's father.

The Lambton story, too, is one of few in which a witch appears. Here the witch advises on the tactics to be used to kill the dragon and exacts a sacrifice as her reward. There are Biblical echoes of the story of King Saul consulting the Witch of Endor. In the story of the Laidly Worm (**178**) the witch is an evil queen and stepmother, capable of transforming humans into monsters by the casting of spells. She seems to be a character straight from Norse mythology, of a type that crops up later in northern fairy tales.

A curious feature of two of the dragon stories is a 'neither-nor' element. Young Lord Lambton is told by the witch, 'Old Elspat of the Glen', to fight his battle with the Lambton worm (**168**) on a rock in the middle of the river Wear – a magical place which was neither land nor water. At Brent

Pelham, in Hertfordshire (**69**), the Devil swears to have the soul of Piers Shonks, the champion who has killed his favourite dragon. To escape that fate Piers instructs that his body be buried in the north wall of the church, which is neither inside nor outside the building.

This theme recurs frequently in the myths and legends of the Celts, Greeks and other Indo-European peoples and may perhaps be present in some of the other dragon stories quoted. Battles take place on the seashore, where land and water meet; they occur at nightfall, when it is neither light nor dark. The same concept is illustrated by the Norse myth of Baldur, who was slain by a dart of mistletoe, a plant which does not have its roots in the soil, like other plants, but lives suspended between earth and sky – a 'neither-nor' plant. And again by the ancient feast of Samhain, now celebrated as Hallowe'en, which is 'neither – nor' territory in which the veil between this world and the world of spirits wears very thin.

MORE THINGS IN HEAVEN AND EARTH...

From the earliest time men have studied the heavens. The oldest prehistoric monuments in Britain, namely Avebury and Stonehenge, seem to have been designed (and with considerable skill) as observatories. Astronomy and its twin, astrology, were well advanced in the early civilisations of Egypt, Mesopotamia, China and other eastern countries, and it shows in their religious mythology: the gods lived in the heavens, to which the eyes of wise men were constantly directed.

Events in the heavens were thought to presage happenings on earth. In particular, unusual manifestations in the skies were associated with natural disasters, such as earthquakes, storms and bad weather but also including riots, plague and famine. In some civilisations the preoccupation with signs in the heavens became almost paranoid. Was there a reason for this?

The much ridiculed and maligned Velikovsky would assert that there was. He it was who put forward the theory that the history of our planet is one of violent jerks and cataclysms rather than a long process of gradual change over millions and millions of years, as orthodox science presents it. Cosmic catastrophism, he calls it. He maintains that the solar system is a macrocosm of the atom. In the atom the electrons that revolve around the nucleus jump about, leaping from one orbit to another when hit by the energy of a photon (light). This happens many times in a second. The same phenomenon occurs in the solar system, declares Velikovsky, only the time-scale is so much vaster. The planets shift their orbits only at irregular intervals, measured by hundreds of thousands of years.

Yet, he insists, they do so leap from orbit to orbit, and the phenomenon has happened at least twice in the past few thousand years. His theory is that the planet Venus was originally a comet which passed close to Earth around the middle of the second millennium BC, causing frightful disturbances.

'We claim', he says in his summary of events, 'that the earth's orbit changed more than once and with it the length of the year; that the geographical position of the terrestrial axis and its astronomical direction changed repeatedly, and that at a recent date the polar star was in the constellation of the Great Bear. The length of day altered; the polar regions shifted, the polar ice became displaced into moderate latitudes, and other regions moved into the polar circles.'

Naturally such drastic changes brought almost incredible destruction to the earth, and most of Velikovsky's book, *Worlds in Collision*, is devoted to an examination of ancient records which, he contends, describe exactly what happened. There are in the ancient literature of nearly all nations and in the folklore of illiterate people references to disastrous earthquakes, days of darkness, hails of stones falling from the sky, hurricanes, tidal waves, reversal of times and seasons and other alarming phenomena. Details of the apocalypse in Norse mythology and in the Book of Revelation may be based on accounts of what actually happened rather than on visions of the future.

From the point of view of this book on dragons, the significant feature is that these terrestrial disasters were accompanied by celestial signs. According to the records of the ancient Babylonians, the solar system consisted of four planets – Jupiter, Saturn, Mars and Mercury. They knew nothing of Venus. This new star suddenly appeared in the heavens as a comet and, after upsetting the entire order of things, eventually settled down in its present orbit as a planet. Men saw it as 'a smoking star', a star with horns, a hairy star, a star which resembled some fearful celestial beast –even, so it is said, as a witch on a broomstick. The peoples of the world, says Velikovsky, saw the events in the sky as 'a fight between an evil monster in the form of a serpent and the light-god who engaged the monster in battle and thus saved the world'. He identifies the comet with Typhon, the monster of Greek mythology, and quotes the description by Apollodorus (c.140 BC) of the battle between Zeus and Typhon: 'Typhon out-topped all the mountains, and his head often brushed the stars. One of his hands reached out to the west and the other to the east, and from them projected a hundred dragon's heads. From the thighs downwards he had huge coils of vipers, which...emitted a long hissing...His body was all winged...and fire flashed from his eyes. Such and so great was Typhon when, hurling kindled rocks, he made for the very heaven with hissing and shouts, spouting a great jet of fire from his mouth.'

Velikovsky comments, 'All around the world the dragon image is prominent in literature and art and also in the religion of peoples. There is probably no nation that does not use this symbol or this creature as an important motif, yet it does not exist...From the description of the comet Typhon that spread like an animal over the sky with its many heads and winged body, with fire flaming from its mouths . . . we recognise the origin of this widespread motif.'

Velikovsky, after many years in the wilderness as a consequence of his startling and unorthodox theories, enjoyed a revived popularity a few years ago when space probes revealed that certain of his predictions about the planet Venus, which were contrary to accepted ideas, were correct. His lecture halls were packed with students. Whether or not we can accept his theories in their entirety, there does seem to be a case for a series of startling events in the heavens, associated with cataclysmic repercussions on earth, though perhaps not at the periods he postulates. That would account for the obsession of peoples all round the world with the stars. Remembering what had happened before, they scanned the heavens anxiously for any signs of the impending recurrence of catastrophe. It seems more reasonable than that they were simply engaged in fixing the dates for sowing, harvesting and the shearing of sheep.

In the light of Velikovsky's emphasis on the significance of events in the heavens, it was inevitable that fervent believers in UFOs should link them with those other mysterious manifestations, flying dragons. The descriptions of flying dragons, say the protagonists of such theories, tally exactly with those of flying saucers, with their glowing lights and erratic trajectories. Dragons are often associated with high places (such as those on which St Michael is said to have vanquished dragons), which are convenient locations for flying saucers to land or at least to be observed. Those who hold that the germs of scientific knowledge have been imparted to the human race by aliens from other worlds can also point out that in ancient mythology the serpent (i.e. the dragon) is the repository of wisdom, as in the story of the Garden of Eden.

As the study of alleged UFOs becomes more intensive it has led some students to regard them as a psychological phenomenon. Like beauty, they are in the eye of the beholder, and only certain people at certain times and in certain places can see them. Compare this theory with the mystery of the Loch Ness monster: despite all the time and ingenuity which has been devoted to investigating Nessie and similar monsters in Scottish and Irish lakes, cameras fail at the critical moment, films do not develop satisfactorily and observers cannot substantiate what they actually saw. Although there is abundant evidence that there is something mysterious in Loch Ness, Loch Morar and the rest, there is also a nebulosity and an elusiveness about the whole concept.

These are abstruse matters on which I do not propose to offer an opinion. I will content myself with quoting a curious incident which I give in my book *The Folklore of Wiltshire.* It takes the form of a letter written by Sir Michael W. S. Bruce to the *Evening Standard* on 23 December 1953: 'Shortly before D-Day I was sent on a course of instruction at Larkhill. Four of us went with an RAF warrant officer in a jeep to select suitable gun sites; we

22. Part of the abundant evidence that something mysterious exists in Loch Ness (**187**): a photograph taken on the loch in May 1977.

Anthony Shiels (Fortean Picture Library)

were coming up from the north towards the road which runs past Stonehenge, and between us and the road lay a small copse. Suddenly we all saw a very small aircraft dive straight down into the wood and disappear in the trees. We raced the jeep up to give assistance; there was no sign of a crash – nothing – nothing flying away to the south. Suddenly I heard the warrant officer shout; he was standing white-faced before a large stone cairn commemorating the first death from an aeroplane accident in this country in 1912.'

Here we have an account of an incident witnessed by five competent and highly reputable observers. Doubt can hardly be cast on its authenticity. The only logical explanation would seem to be that, under certain conditions not yet understood but involving certain times, places and perhaps persons, the veil between past and present (and perhaps future) wears very thin, enabling observers to slip temporarily into a different time.

By implication, any baffling visual phenomenon could be explained by a time slip. Were the brilliant dragons of Penllin (**105**) really folk memories passed down through the centuries or did some gifted Welsh observer not so very long ago catch a glimpse of the banners which accompanied a Roman army? Were at least some of the vivid descriptions of dragons, perhaps some of those incorporated in mediaeval carvings and paintings, based on brief visions of carnivorous dinosaurs which once, ages ago, occupied space in what is now England's green and pleasant land? Perhaps in the future we shall learn more, but for the present, who can say?

Gazetteer

Pre-1971 county boundaries have generally been followed for England and Scotland, but not for Wales, thus:

County	Dragon nos.	County	Dragon nos.
Angus	184	Leics	118–20
Argyll	185–6	Lincs	123–6
Beds	78	London	43–4
Berks	46–8	Man, Isle of	150–3
Bucks	67–8	Norfolk	84–8
Cheshire	139–41	Northants	90–1
Clwyd	142	Northumberland	178–80
Cornwall	1–4	Notts	127–9
Cumberland	176–7	Orkney	191–2
Derbys	130–8	Oxon	62–6
Devon	5–10	Powys	111–12
Dorset	25–6	Ross & Cromarty	189
Durham	168–73	Roxburgh	181
Dyfed	108–10	Rutland	121–2
Essex	38–42	Shetland	193–4
Glamorgan	105–7	Shropshire	113–14
Gloucs	55–61	Somerset	11–24
Gwynnedd	143–9	Staffs	115–17
Hants	27–30	Suffolk	79–83
Hereford	100–4	Surrey	45
Herts	69–77	Sussex	32–6
Hunts	89	Sutherland	190
Inverness	187–8	Warwicks	92–4
Jersey	31	Westmorland	174–5
Kent	37	Wilts	49–54
Kirkcudbright	182–3	Worcs	95–9
Lancs	154	Yorks	155–67

CORNWALL

1. Padstow

One glance at the Padstow oss is enough to arouse doubts as to whether it really is supposed to be a horse. It doesn't look like one. Its body consists of a highly decorated tarpaulin or drape stretched over a hoop-like frame. The upper parts of the bearer are covered by a black cape, and the man is rendered anonymous by a grotesque mask.

The oss is the chief character in the May Day festivities at Padstow, which start at midnight and carry on all day. Accompanied by a club-bearer, known as the Teaser, and a group of attendants, it prances around the streets of the little town. In former times it made an excursion to Treator Pool, outside the town, ostensibly for refreshment, but as the journey was considered too far the Golden Lion hostelry now serves as a substitute. At Treator Pool it used to sprinkle onlookers with water for good luck. It also tried to catch any girls it encountered and drag them under its canopy. They would emerge well smeared with soot and, it is said, with the assurance that they would have a baby within a year.

A feature of the parade is that from time to time the oss sinks, apparently dying, to the ground. Then the Teaser strikes it lightly with his club, whereupon the oss is restored to life and vigour and, to a lively jig, goes prancing on its way.

Padstow has a second oss, the Blue Ribbon or Temperance oss, probably introduced in late Victorian times as a protest against the beer-drinking associated with the official oss.

Originally, the oss was probably the representation of a potent fertility god. What sort of creature it is really supposed to portray is open to debate, but it is obviously closely related to Snap, the Norwich dragon (**85**), and so earns a place in this book. See also page 26.

The docile dragon. The story of St Carantoc and the docile dragon of Carhampton (**16**) is sometimes associated with St Petroc, presumably at Padstow. Apart from the change of venue, the details are almost identical. With his girdle around the subdued dragon's neck,

> 'St Petroc led the docile creature down
> To the sandy seashore, where amid the waves
> The last great Cornish dragon swam away,
> Bound for what strand or desert island far
> We none of us can tell...'

2. Helston

Helston's famous Furry Dance is said to have originated as a celebration of St Michael's victory over the Devil. Built into a wall of the Angel Hotel is a large granite boulder, known as Hell's Stone because it used to block the gateway to Hell. In the fight with St Michael, the Devil picked up this stone and hurled it at the saint, fortunately missing him. The story features here because during the battle the Devil took the form of a dragon and when defeated, flew away and took refuge in a lake.

3. Egloskerry

In Egloskerry church is the sculpture of a dragon with a three-forked tail.

4. Tremain

Tremain church also has a carving of a dragon.

DEVON

5. Exe Valley

This dragon is supposed to haunt the two Iron Age hill forts of Dolbury Hill and Cadbury Hill, situated on opposite sides of the Exe Valley, just north of Exeter. Great treasures are hidden in one or both of these ancient castles, guarded by the dragon who flies from one to the other at night. Of the treasures a local rhyme states:

'If Cadbury Castle and Dolbury Hill delven were
All England might plough with a golden share.'

6. Manaton

The Manaton dragon seems to have been a kind of flying serpent. Its trunk was the size of a man's. It possessed legs and wings and was frequently to be seen flying around. Its hissing could be heard for miles. Its lair was an old Dartmoor tin-mine, near which it is reputed to have been killed. A late eighteenth-century writer, Polwhele, who recorded the story, seems not to have believed it.

On the moors near the dragon's lair are numerous hut circles, dating from the Bronze Age and including a group of twenty-four within a walled enclosure. The local name for the enclosure is Grimspound, 'Grim' evidently referring to a giant or devil.

23. Grimspound, the Bronze Age enclosure near which the Manaton dragon (**6**) is said to have had its lair.

7. Challacombe

The Challacombe dragons once lived on or near certain 'hillocks of earth' at Challacombe, on Exmoor. They were fiery, winged creatures which could be seen flying around and alighting on the 'Hillocks', which are groups of barrows, probably of the Bronze Age, on the high moors.

8. Winkleigh

These dragons were mentioned by two Devonshire writers of the seventeenth century, but nothing further is known about them. We do not even know how many there were – just that they are referred to in the plural.

9. Combe Martin

Combe Martin, on the North Devon coast, once possessed a hobby horse, possibly derived from a dragon and very similar to the Minehead hobby horse (**23**) and the Padstow oss (**1**).

10. Down St Mary
A dragon, flanking a human and a dog, is depicted on a tympanum in the church here.

SOMERSET

11. Crowcombe
Crowcombe, a pleasant little village under the Quantock Hills, had a celebrated dragon, the Crowcombe worm, which lived in Shervage Wood. It is described as having a body thicker than the trunks of three oak trees. After preying for a time on ponies and sheep, it began to turn its attention to humans and became such a nuisance that everyone was afraid to go near the wood. This was a serious deprivation, for Shervage Wood was noted for bilberries, and bilberry pie was a famous local dish.

One old woman, who had formerly made a living out of making and selling bilberry pies, met a woodcutter from Stogumber, a mile or two away, and, suspecting that he would not know about the worm, persuaded him to go into the wood and gather bilberries for her. The kind-hearted woodcutter agreed and by lunchtime had picked a hatful. When he sat down on a log to enjoy his lunch of bread and cheese and cider, the log started to wriggle. Realising that he was sitting on a living monster, he seized his axe and chopped the creature in half before it could properly wake up. What he did not know was that the two ends were capable of joining up again. However, he was lucky, for the dragon was so disorientated that one end began to slither south towards Taunton while the other wriggled off towards Minehead. So the Crowcombe worm died.

When he came out of the wood and handed the hatful of bilberries to the old woman, she enquired whether he had had any trouble.

'Oh, only a little, with an old dragon,' he replied off-handedly.

'Oh, did you see the dragon?' she said. 'Didn't you know it was there? I'm surprised no one ever told you about it.'

'I was told about it,' he assured her, 'by a Crowcombe woman. But I took no notice of it, because everybody knows that all Crowcombe people are liars!'

The inference is that, as the story of the Crowcombe worm comes from Crowcombe, you can believe it or not!

The killing of the Crowcombe worm is commemorated by a carved

J C D Smith

24. The bench-end in Crowcombe church which depicts the
killing of the Crowcombe worm (**11**).

bench-end of the early sixteenth century in Crowcombe church. The details do not, however, correspond with the legend. The dragon has two heads, one growing out from its belly, and is being slain by two men who are thrusting spears into one of its throats.

12. Kingston St Mary

A particularly fierce dragon is said to have lived near the village of Kingston St Mary, just north of Taunton. After committing many depredations it was challenged by a hero who stood outside its lair, taunting it. When the dragon opened its mouth to roar, the champion rolled in a great boulder, which choked it. Ruth Tongue, who recorded the story, says that her informant pointed out the spot on a hillside from which the hero dislodged the stone. Told in the Somerset vernacular, it relates that: 'there was a bold veller as had a good head on him, and he climbed a lane by Ivyton where there was a gurt rock in those days. 'Tis a steep hill, look, and rock was right on brow, so he gave a shout to dragon. Well then, dragon he do look up and sees 'en. Then he opens his gurt mouth to roar vlames, and the veller gives the rock a shove-off. It rolled straight down hill into dragon's mouth and choked 'n dead. Yes, it did.'

13. Norton Fitzwarren

The dragon of Norton Fitzwarren, a village which has now become almost a suburb of Taunton, had its home in the Iron Age fort on the hill above the town. At some unknown date in the past a battle is said to have raged here, and the dragon was generated from the heaps of decomposing corpses. In due course it developed predatory habits, terrorising the countryside until the people persuaded a knightly champion, Fulk Fitzwarine, to kill it.

The event is said to be commemorated in a rood screen in Norton Fitzwarren church. A splendid example of wood carving, it is the work of a known artist, Ralph Harris, who died in 1509 and is buried in the church. Though covered in the early eighteenth century by oak stain, the figures were originally brightly painted and some of the colours show through. The dragon is a lively-looking creature, black with a gold stripe down its back, and is apparently eating a naked lady. Two men are depicted but do not seem to be doing much about rescuing the girl; one is evidently running away. There is no sign of Fulk Fitzwarine, the dragon-killer.

Fulk himself is an historical person of the thirteenth century who fell foul of King John and was in consequence exiled. Overseas he continued to follow the pursuit of dragon-killer, for one of his exploits was to rescue the

25. This fine example of early sixteenth-century wood-carving on a rood screen in Norton Fitzwarren church is said to portray the celebrated local dragon (**13**).

daughter of the Duke of Iberia from the den of a dragon near Carthage. This dragon slept on a bed of gold, which cooled its hot blood, so when Fulk slew it he acquired the gold and came home rich.

14. Aller

Aller is the village on the edge of the Somerset marshes where in the year 878 King Alfred triumphantly presented the Danish leader, Guthrum, whom he had recently defeated at the battle of Ethandune, for baptism as a Christian convert. If it had not been for this episode modern historians would have had no evidence of the existence of Aller until the time of the Domesday Book.

At what period Aller's dragon lived is not known, but it is said to have had its lair in the side of a hill near Aller, from which it made frequent forays into the neighbouring parishes.

There are several versions of the story of its depredations and demise.

The dragon was said to have been a great flying serpent covered with scales. Crops and trees were poisoned by its breath, which was so foul that humans could hardly endure it. Like some other dragons, it had particular liking for milk and often sent milkmaids flying in terror when it descended to drink the contents of their pails.

The hero who eventually killed it was known as John of Aller. In some versions he is called a knight, in others he is regarded as an ordinary villager. His armour for the combat was a coat of pitch, and a mask as protection from the dragon's breath. He was armed with a long spear specially made for the encounter, and with this he attacked the dragon while it was sleeping in its den. After a desperate battle the dragon was killed. John of Aller then found that there were two or three baby dragons in the cave so he went home for a harrow, with which he got his labourers to block the entrance. This detail is apparently included to explain a tradition that 'the dragon of Aller was slain by a harrow'.

As confirmatory evidence we are referred to the spear with which John killed the dragon. It is about nine feet long and is to be seen in the church at Low Ham, though originally it was kept in the belfry at Aller. In Aller church, too, there is a damaged effigy of a knight said to be John of Aller.

One version of the story places the den of the dragon at Curry Rivel, on the far side of the marshes. It used to fly across to commit its outrages at Aller, however, and the hero who slew it was the same John of Aller. In this version John lay in ambush for it and fought it with a sword, with which he at last cut off the monster's head. He was badly burned by the dragon's fiery breath and died at the same moment as the dragon. The site of the battle was so scorched that thereafter no grass would grow on it. When this story was written down by a folklorist in 1885, the local farmer who related it was able to point out the bare patch. According to this version, John was so admired that the village was named after him, not vice versa.

15. Kilve

Kilve, on the Bristol Channel coast, had a dragon named Blue Ben. He lived in Outsham Hill and used to go down regularly to the sea to cool himself. One reason for this behaviour was that the Devil used to harness him and ride him round the streets of Hell, which were too hot even for a dragon. He built a causeway of rocks extending out to sea, so that he could plunge off it into deeper water. One day, however, while hastening across this causeway he slipped into the surrounding mud and was drowned. His skull was retrieved and is now to be seen in Taunton Museum.

However, the skull is that of a fossilised ichthyosaurus and the story is thought to be of fairly modern invention, not a genuine item of folklore.

16. Carhampton

The story of this dragon illustrates an alternative method of dealing with dragons, other than killing them. It concerns a Celtic saint, Carantoc, who arrived on the Somerset coast having floated over from Wales with his altar. The story begins with Carantoc looking for his altar, and King Arthur looking for a fiery dragon which he had heard was making a nuisance of itself.

It seems that King Arthur knows the whereabouts of the altar and offers to reveal it on condition that Carantoc undertakes to get rid of the dragon. This is not exactly the kind of bargain one would expect from a champion looking for a dragon to kill, but that is how the story goes. Carantoc retires to pray and soon the dragon arrives, roaring. The saint puts his stole round its neck and leads it away like a lamb. When Carantoc takes the dragon into the king's castle, some of the people are frightened and try to kill it, but Carantoc does not allow that. He takes it to the castle gate and there releases it, telling it to go away and never return.

As a reward for his intervention, Carantoc was granted a stretch of land which has been identified as Carhamptom. The castle is supposed to be Dunster, and the dragon's den Ker Moor.

The story is apparently linked with the Minehead hobby horse (**23**), which itself is probably a derivation from a dragon. On its annual perambulations, the Minehead horse has to visit certain places, among them Dunster Castle and a place called Dragon's Cross.

It may or may not be significant that Carhamptom is one of the few places in the West Country where the annual mid-winter ceremony of wassailing the apple trees is still observed.

See also the docile dragon of Padstow (**1**), and page 55.

17. Churchstanton

Little is known of the Churchstanton dragon. It lived long ago on what is now Stapley Farm and, after committing the usual atrocities, was killed by an anonymous 'valiant knight'. The site of its den and of its demise is a field known as Wormstall, 'worm' being a synonym for 'dragon'. A hollow still visible is said to have been made by its lashing tail as it expired.

18. Trull

A brief mention exists of a dragon who lived and was killed on Castleman's Hill, near Trull.

In the church of Trull, appropriately dedicated to St Michael, a stained glass window portrays St Michael, St George and St Margaret of Antioch, each killing a dragon.

19. Lullington

Here dragons are depicted in a church sculpture, devouring the Life Tree.

20. Flax Bourton

This unfortunate beast is shown on a Norman tympanum in Flax Bourton church, being slain by St Michael who is thrusting a cross down its throat.

21. Cleeve

The carved dragon in Cleeve church may portray the dragon tamed by St Carantoc at Carhampton (**16**), not far away.

22. St Decumans

A similar dragon carving, with perhaps the same origin, is to be seen in the church of St Decumans.

23. Minehead

The Minehead hobby horse resembles the Padstow oss (**1**) and, like it, is associated with May Day festivities. Each town claims to have the original oss and accuses the other of stealing the idea. As at Padstow, osses have proliferated. Minehead now has three, all very similar. They have boat-shaped rather than round bodies, draped in cloth, and the bearer is masked. Each is equipped with a cow's tail with which it lashes about, catching unwary spectators a stinging blow. The Town Horse, one of the three, is accompanied by a party of attendants, known as Gullivers, and by a band in which drums and accordions chiefly feature. During the day the horse or horses make the journey to Dunster, and on other days of the week they visit the neighbouring villages of Periton and Cher.

One of the horses is the property of the Fishermen's Guild, and some folklorists have linked this with their resemblance to boats rather than horses. There is, however, a distinct resemblance to Snap, the Norwich dragon (**85**), which can qualify them for inclusion in a book of dragons.

Nicholas Servian FIIP. Woodmansterne Ltd

26. A misericord from Wells Cathedral (**24**).

24. Wells

Misericords in Wells Cathedral show a left-handed man slaying a wyvern; also a baby dragon tucking its head under its wing.

DORSET

25. Poundbury

Approaching Dorchester from the north-west, along the A37 road, one sees on the south side of the valley the imposing earthen ramparts of Poundbury which is often taken to be Maiden Castle. The two Iron Age fortresses are, in fact, quite distinct; Maiden Castle lies a couple of miles to the south, and is best approached from the Dorchester–Weymouth road. The valley dominated by Poundbury is that of the little river Frome, now occupied by fertile water-meadows but once, according to tradition, by an extensive lake, inhabited by monsters. What these monsters were like or whether they were true dragons, no one knows.

26. Wynford Eagle

A carving in the churtch of Wynford Eagle shows two dragons fighting.

Aerofilms

27. The water-meadows on the left of the picture, beneath the earthen ramparts of Poundbury Castle (**25**), near Dorchester, were said once to have been a monster-infected lake.

Dorset Natural History and Archaeological Society

28. The dragon carving in the church of Wynford Eagle (**26**).

HAMPSHIRE

27. Bisterne

The Bisterne dragon seems to have been a rather likeable creature. Its lair was on Burley Beacon, a hill in the New Forest, and, according to one version of the story, it took to coming over to Bisterne every day for a bucket of milk. It was because the villagers grew tired of paying this tribute that they eventually destroyed the dragon.

They hired a knight named Sir Macdonie de Berkeley to be their champion. His chosen weapons were a sword, a large jug of milk and a glass case. Near the dragon's den he poured the milk into a row of cans, retreated to the glass case and waited. In due course the dragon came down and started to lap the milk. When it was thoroughly preoccupied, Sir Macdonie stepped out and killed it.

Another version makes the dragon a much more fearsome creature, addicted to the flesh of cattle and humans rather than existing on a milk diet. Its ravages became so outrageous that the villagers persuaded a famous knight, Sir Maurice de Berkeley, to deal with it. He did so by the ruse, known to other dragon-killers, of covering his armour with bird-lime and powdered glass. In the battle two large dogs which assisted the knight were killed and Sir Maurice himself was so exhausted that he died soon afterwards. It is said that he refused to discuss the battle with anyone.

The great fight occurred in a field known as Dragon Field. It is placed in the reign of Edward IV (1461–83) who granted the champion the right to wear a dragon on his coat of arms. A stone dragon still adorns the entrance to Bisterne Park, while sculptures of the dogs, which are of the mastiff type, stand on adjacent terraces. And the former village inn at Bisterne was, according to the 1867 edition of the Post Office Directory, called The George & Dragon, though according to other sources The Green Dragon.

There is a connection between this legend and that of Deerhurst in Gloucestershire (**57**), for the Berkeley family, who produced the hero of the Bisterne story, came originally from the neighbourhood of Deerhurst. A document in the possession of the Berkeley family, dated before 1618 and preserved in the family archives in Berkeley Castle, refers to the Bisterne dragon-killer as 'Sir Moris Barkley, the sonne of Sir John Barkley of Beverston, being a man of great strength and great courage'. This document seems to refute the statement that the combat took place in the reign of Edward IV, for it refers to Sir Moris bearing a 'Miter' with a dragon crest in the year 1431, in the reign of Henry VI. If the Sir Moris

Barkley of the story is the historical Sir Maurice Berkeley of Bisterne who held important offices in Southampton, it is known that his death occurred in 1460.

28. Wherwell

Wherwell's cockatrice seems to have been a kind of dragon. It was hatched from a duck egg, incubated by a toad, in a cellar beneath Wherwell Priory. The nuns, regarding it as a curiosity, made a pet of it at first, but after a time it became unmanageable. It took to flying around the village, terrorising the inhabitants, and was not averse to picking up a stray human and eating him or her.

Obviously it had to be stopped, so a reward of four acres of land was offered to anyone who would kill the monster. Several champions came to try, but all lost their lives in the adventure. Eventually salvation came from near at hand. A Priory servant named Green devised an ingenious plan for dealing with the cockatrice, which was evidently still living in the cellar where it had been born. He lowered a highly polished steel mirror into the cockatrice's lair, and the monster, seeing its own reflection and thinking that its territory was being invaded by another cockatrice, attacked. When it was nearly dropping with exhaustion, Green stepped down and killed it with a spear.

We know what this cockatrice looked like, for a cockatrice weather-vane was made for the steeple of St Peter and Holy Cross at Wherwell and is now preserved in Andover Museum. It has the head, beak, wings and talons of a predatory bird, but an elongated, scaly body like that of a wyvern, ending in an arrow-shaped tail. See also page 54.

There are other circumstantial details which could be taken as confirmation of the story. In nearby Harewood Forest is a plot of land, measuring exactly four acres, known as Green's Acres. And the Women's Institute publication, *It Happened in Hampshire*, compiled in the 1930s, testifies that 'none of the older generation of inhabitants could be induced to eat a duck's egg'!

29. Highclere

Little is known of the Highclere grampus, except that it could not have been the sort of grampus known to modern zoologists, which is a kind of dolphin. The Highclere grampus lived in a giant yew near the old church, emerging from time to time to terrify the villagers. Betweentimes they could hear it wheezing and coughing in its leafy den.

They enlisted the aid of the vicar, who exorcised the monster, banishing it by bell, book and candle to the Red Sea for a thousand years. The twist in the tail of the story is that, as no one knows when the event occurred, the thousand years may be up at any time and then the grampus will be back again! See also pages 40–41.

30. Yateley
In the Yateley mumming play King George (alias St George) boasts that he 'fought the fiery dragon' and so won the King of Egypt's daughter.

JERSEY

31. La Hogue Bie
The dragon in this story plays a subsidiary role. Presumably it committed sufficient mischief to cause the local people to demand that it be dealt with. So the lord of the manor, the Seigneur de Hambye, engaged the dragon in straightforward single combat and succeeded in killing it. While he was resting, exhausted, after the fight, his squire crept up and murdered him. The squire then returned to the village, announcing that, after his master had been killed, he himself had slain the dragon. As his reward he demanded the right to marry his master's widow and thus, of course, to acquire his estates. His story was at first believed and the marriage was celebrated. Soon afterwards, however, he began to have nightmares and to talk in his sleep. His horrified bride pieced together the truth and in the end he confessed.

The story is associated with a tumulus, which is said to be the grave of the Seigneur.

SUSSEX

Sussex has the advantage of being the home province of one of the most able and indefatigable of folklorists, Jacqueline Simpson, who in the course of her researches has thoroughly investigated the Sussex dragons.

29. The knucker of Lyminster (**32**), near Arundel, was a water monster who lived in this reputedly bottomless pool known as the Knucker Hole.

32. Lyminster

The Lyminster knucker, one of the best-known of English dragons, was a water monster. It lived in a deep pool by the church at Lyminster, near Arundel. Tradition claimed that the pool, known as the Knucker Hole, which is one of several similar ones which formerly existed in the vicinity, is bottomless, though it is in fact about thirty feet deep. Fed by underground springs, it never dries up and never freezes in winter. Apparently the other pools were also known as Knucker Holes, so we seem to have a local generic name for a race of water monsters.

The Lyminster knucker followed the usual pattern of behaviour of dragons, terrorising the countryside and seizing cattle and people to carry off to its watery lair. In one version it had a particular liking for maidens and so depleted the local supply that eventually only one was left, the daughter of the King of Sussex. The royal father was so distressed that he offered the daughter in marriage to anyone who would slay the knucker.

At least three versions of the killing of the knucker survive, and all give the hero a different identity.

The first is a wandering knight who happened to pass that way. He engaged in a conventional battle with the knucker, slew it and claimed the princess as his bride. In the 1880s local residents could point out his tombstone in the churchyard, and some of them claimed him and the princess as their ancestors. As circumstantial evidence they pointed to a sword resting on a herring-bone pattern on the gravestone, asserting that it depicted the hero's sword resting on the dragon's ribs. In fact, the tomb is probably that of a Crusader, the herring-bone pattern being a convention at that time. It used to lie in the churchyard but has now been moved into the church.

The second version identifies the hero as a local lad named Jim Puttock. It has the advantage of having been written down exactly as told by a hedger, and was published in the *Sussex County Magazine* in 1929 (pp. 845–6). The details of the story are more prosaic. The reward is offered not by the King of Sussex but by the Mayor of Arundel. The knucker causes trouble not only by snapping up cows and horses and people, 'licking 'em up, like a toad licking flies off a stone', but also by 'swimming in the river otherwhile and sticking his ugly face up again the winders in Shipyard when people was sitting having their tea'. Jim Puttock, the dragon-killer, is 'a young chap from Wick'.

Jim Puttock's chosen weapon is a pudding. According to the article in the *Sussex County Magazine* referred to, he obtains a 'gert iron pot' from the blacksmith, a quantity of flour from the miller, a huge stack of firewood from the woodman. Having made 'the biggest pudden that was ever seen', he has it hoisted on a timber-wagon, drawn by a team of horses. The knucker sees it coming and enquires what it is.

'"Pudden," says Jim.

'"Pudden?" says the dragon. "What be that?"

'"Just you try," says Jim.

'And he didn't want no more telling – pudden, horses, tug, they was gone in a blink.'

The knucker agrees that it was a tasty titbit and says he would like another. Jim Puttock promises to bring him one in the afternoon. Before that, however, a great commotion occurs. It is the knucker suffering from indigestion. When Jim goes back in the afternoon the knucker roars, 'Don't you dare bring me no more o' that there pudden, young man!'

'"Why?" says Jim. "What's matter?"

'"Collywobbles," says the dragon. "It do set so heavy on me I can't stand up, nowhows in the wurreld.'

'"Shouldn't bolt it so," says Jim. "But never mind. I got a pill here, soon cure that."

'"Where?" says the knucker.

'"Here," says Jim. And he ups with an axe he'd held behind his back, and cuts off his head.'

Once again the same gravestone offers circumstantial evidence of the story. Local tradition says that beneath it lies the mortal remains of 'the man who killed the dragon'.

The third version is similar in main outline, though the details differ. The hero, a farmer's boy, is named Jim Pulk. He prepares a huge pie or pudding which he takes on a farm cart to the Knucker Hole, leaving it there and lying in wait behind a hedge. The knucker makes a meal of the pie, cart, horse and all but shortly afterwards lies down and dies. This is because Jim Pulk has poisoned the pie. Jim emerges from his hiding-place, cuts off the dragon's head with a scythe and goes back to the village to celebrate.

There then occurs a twist to the story resembling the sequels to dragon-killing in other places. 'He went down to the Six Bells Inn, had a drink to celebrate his victory, and fell down dead. Presumably he had got some poison on his hand which, no doubt, very probably, he drew across his mouth after downing his pint.'

The gravestone attached to the hero of this story is the one associated with the knight in the first version. Jacqueline Simpson mentions that at least one child in the 1930s used to decorate the stone with snapdragons.

The common feature of the stories of Jim Puttock and Jim Pulk, the giant pudding, was also a somewhat notorious feature of rural life in the first half of the nineteenth century, and probably earlier, too. Consisting almost entirely of flour and water, it was highly indigestible, especially when cold. In the story of Jim Puttock the teller brings in a graphic detail when describing the preparation of the 'pudden': 'When 'twas done – not that 'twas quite done – bit sad in the middle, I reckon, but that was all the better, like ...' one gathers that he knew about 'Sussex pudden' from experience, as farm workers used to take it to the fields with them for lunch.

33. St Leonard's Forest

St Leonard's Forest, near Horsham, is a part of the ancient forest of the Weald, which retained its wild, almost impenetrable character until quite recent times – the sort of place where dragons and other strange creatures might be expected. In the thirteenth century a chapel in the forest was dedicated to St Leonard, who was in fact a Frankish hermit who lived in the sixth century and achieved fame by persuading King Clovis of the Franks to release some prisoners of war. After a time local people began to assume that St Leonard had actually lived in the forest and so was credited with killing a dragon which had its residence there. A circumstantial detail was that where the saint's blood, spilled in the desperate fight, soaked the ground patches of lilies-of-the-valley sprang up (though some say that it was the dragon's blood which encouraged their growth).

There is a subsidiary legend that, as a reward for the saint's courage, adders were banished from the forest or at least deprived of their venom, and also that nightingales were sent into exile, because their singing had disturbed the saint at his prayers.

Was there a dragon legend associated with the forest at an earlier date, whose hero became identified with St Leonard when he appeared on the scene? We cannot know. Jacqueline Simpson quotes the name of one of the forest villages, Dragon's Green, which sounds suggestive, but she points out that a local estate was in 1296 owned by a family named Dragons. All is very obscure.

However, the situation is enlivened by the alleged appearance of a dragon there in August 1614. The event is recorded in a pamphlet still surviving and is quoted in several books on Sussex and the Weald.

The dragon, or serpent, was said to be 'nine feete or rather more in length, and shaped almost in the forme of an axletree of a cart; a quantitie of thickness in the middest, and somewhat smaller at both endes. The former part, which he shootes forth as a necke, is supposed to be an elle long; with a white ring, as it were, of scales about it. The scales along his backe seem to be blackish, and so much as is discovered under his bellie, appeareth to be red ... There are likewise upon either side of him discovered, two great bunches so big as a large foote-ball, and (so some thinke) will in time grow to wings; but God, I hope, will that he shall be destroyed before he grow to fledge.'

The pamphlet goes on to describe how a man and a woman were killed by the dragon's venom 'cast about four rodde from him', and also how a man who set out with his two mastiffs to hunt it saw the two dogs killed and was lucky to escape with his life. However, neither the people nor the dogs were eaten by the monster, who was thought to have preyed on rabbits from a warren in the vicinity. Wherever the dragon went it left behind a trail of 'glutinous and slimie matter' like a snail's, which gave off an offensive smell.

The haunt of this dragon was near a place called Faygate, but it had been seen at various localities within three or four miles, once within half a mile of Horsham. The observers who claimed to have seen the monster were John Steele, Christopher Holder, and 'a widow woman dwelling neare Faygate'. They also stated that 'the carrier of Horsham, who lieth at the White Horse in Southwark' could testify to the truth of their statement.

A possible explanation of this curious episode can be found on page 56.

34. Cissbury

Cissbury, a commanding height crowned by a prehistoric earthwork on the South Downs above Worthing, is reputed to hold an enormous treasure in a tunnel leading from it to Offington Hall, a distance of about two miles. In the 1860s it is said that the owner of the hall offered half the treasure to anyone who would uncover it by clearing out the passage. Several people who attempted to were driven back by large snakes which, they said, sprang at them hissing, with open mouths.

30. Cissbury (**34**), a prehistoric earthwork on a hilltop near Worthing, is said to have beneath it an immense treasure in a tunnel guarded by monstrous serpents.

Aerofilms

This episode is fairly recent, but it seems that the tradition of the 'monstrous serpents' has an earlier origin. It is interesting that Cissbury has legendary associations with both fairies and the Devil.

35. Bignor

Little information survives about the Bignor dragon or serpent, which lived on Bignor Hill. The imprints of its coils were, it was alleged, to be seen winding around the hill, but these seem to have been no more than familiar paths made by sheep following the contours.

36. Fittleworth

This monster serpent was heard of as recently as 1867, when a folklorist reported that the villagers were frightened of it. It would, they said, rush out hissing at anyone who passed its den.

KENT

37. The Hooden Horse

The Hooden Horse of Kent was a character in a number of mumming plays formerly performed in the county. It seems to have been a nondescript creature, resembling a dragon as much as a horse. It is included here because in recent years the plays have been revived in Folkestone and Tunbridge Wells, among other places.

ESSEX

38. Henham

We owe our information about this monster to an author, thought to be Robert Winstanley of Saffron Walden, who wrote a pamphlet entitled *A True Relation of a Monstrous Serpent seen at Henham on the Mount in Saffron Walden*, which was published in Clerkenwell in 1669. What are supposed to be eye-witness accounts of its appearance in May of that year describe it as a flying serpent, as thick as a man's leg, eight or nine feet long and having eyes as big as a sheep's, sharp teeth and small wings. The story has

31. The flying serpent of Henham (**38**) is said to have been chased away from the village in the seventeenth century by villagers armed with farm tools and stones.

no conquering hero and the serpent seems to have been a relatively innocuous creature. It was eventually chased away by village men armed with farm implements and stones. Five years later advertisements appear for a fair 'to be held at Henham for the sale of Flying Serpents', which were models, and this event continued annually until 1939. The episode attracted enough attention for two London pubs to be named 'The Essex Serpent', and a local beer sold in the village was called 'Snakebite'! There is a suspicion that the whole story is a romance got up as a publicity exercise.

However, there is in St Mary's church, Henham, a mediaeval carving of a dragon, and some modern writers think the story to be not without foundation, though just what kind of creature was involved is difficult to imagine.

39. Horndon

Few details are known of this serpent. It was said to have been imported, at some date in the Middle Ages, by Barbary merchants and to have escaped into the woods around Horndon. There it was eventually killed by a knight, Sir James Tyrell, who adopted the tactics practised by other dragon-killers of wearing armour so highly polished that the dragon could see its reflection in it. Or perhaps the purpose of the polish was to dazzle the dragon. See also page 65.

40. St Osyth

A broadsheet produced in 1704 referred to an occasion, in the reign of Henry II, when 'a dragon of marvellous bigness was discovered at St Osyth, in Essex'. The reference would seem to be to the skeleton of some prehistoric creature. See also page 18.

41. Heybridge

This is one of the parishes known, from church accounts, to have had a dragon effigy in the late Middle Ages. There is a record of it being repaired in 1517.

42. Saffron Walden

The pamphlet of 1669 which deals with the Henham serpent (**38**) also relates the story of the cockatrice of Saffron Walden. 'One of these most venomous Serpents in former times lurked about the meads near Saffron Walden in Essex, who by his very sight killed so many as the Town became almost depopulated.'

The description of this cockatrice is curious, and readers may like to compare it with the Wherwell cockatrice (**28**): 'It is not above a foot in length, of colour between black and yellow, having very red eyes, a sharp head and a white spot hereon like a Crown. It goeth not winding like other Serpents but upright on his breast.' It is not hard to visualise it. One would not expect such a small creature to be dangerous, but 'if a man touch it though with a long pole it kills him: and if it sees a man a far off it destroys him with its looks'. Furthermore 'it breaketh stones, blasteth all Plants with his breath, it burneth everything it goeth over; no herb can grow near the place of his abode'.

The cockatrice was slain by a 'valerous Knight' who, much as Sir James Tyrell in dealing with the Horndon serpent (**39**), dressed himself in a 'coat of christall glass'. This accoutrement seems to have had a deleterious effect on the cockatrice, who 'suddenly dyed'. The knight hung his sword in Walden church as a memorial. Brass effigies were made of the cockatrice and also set up in the church, together with a tablet relating the story. All these relics survived until the Civil War, when they were smashed by Parliamentarian soldiers.

Howard C Moore. Woodmansterne Ltd

32. A thirteenth-century carved wooden boss from Westminster Abbey
(**43**).

LONDON

43. Westminster Abbey

On a carved wooden boss in Westminster Abbey a dragon is seen in combat
with a centaur, who is half-man and half-lion. It dates from the middle of
the thirteenth century.

Westminster had a dragon, or rather a number of dragons in the late
Middle Ages, for the churchwardens' account books of St Margaret's make
occasional references to them. These effigies were evidently hired out to
neighbouring parishes for processions and festivals, for an entry of 1491
records a fee received from St Sepulchre's 'for the Dragon'. In 1502 one
Michell Wosebyche received a fee 'for mayking of VIII Dragons'.

44. City of London

Dragons support the arms of the City
of London, and lively sculptures of
dragons mark the boundary of the City
at several points, one of them being on
the Embankment near the Temple.

33. This impressive dragon marks
a boundary point of the City of
London (**44**). Dragons support the
arms of the City.

Popperfoto

SURREY

45. Buckland

Buckland, at the foot of the North Downs, was the somewhat unlikely possessor of a shag, which is described as a kind of water monster. The Lyminster knucker (**32**) seems to have been a similar creature, so perhaps the Buckland shag also had a deep pool to live in, though its feeding-place was a rock which is said still to bear the bloodstains of its victims. No physical battle took place with this dragon, but the Vicar of Buckland was successful in banishing it, by bell, book and candle, to the Red Sea – the same fate as befell the Highclere grampus (**29**).

BERKSHIRE

46. White Horse Hill

The white horse carved on White Horse Hill near Uffington does not look like a horse. In another book I have likened it to a furtive alley cat slinking up over the brow, and I stand by that description. Although it closely resembles the stylised horses with beaked heads depicted on Celtic coins, suggestions that it is supposed to be a dragon are worth consideration.

The figure is carved on the edge of an escarpment facing west-north-west and is not in the best position to be seen from below in the immediate vicinity. It is best viewed from a distance or from the air. It portrays an animal in full gallop, with its head rather higher than its tail, as though it is moving obliquely uphill, going westwards.

Its hill forms a kind of amphitheatre and is marked by certain terraces called the Giant's Stairs. Detached from it but in a pivotal position is a small, circular, flat-topped hill with the significant name of Dragon Hill. Here, says a local legend, St George fought with and slew the dragon. On the summit of the hill is a patch of bare ground where no grass will grow, according to tradition, because the dragon's blood poisoned the soil.

When the horse was being restored after the camouflage necessary during the Second World War, the contractors pointed out to me a place on the side of the main hill from which it was possible to converse in a normal voice with men working on the opposite hillside, perhaps a quarter of a mile away. The terrain served as a gigantic whispering gallery.

Down in the Vale of the White Horse, in a garden in the village of

Kingston Lisle, stands a great boulder, riddled with holes like an Emmenthal cheese and known as the Blowing Stone. If you blow hard into the right hole a great, booming, hollow note is sounded. The Blowing Stone, said the owner of the garden, had not always stood in his garden. It had been moved down from the hill, somewhere near the horse. My suspicion is that its true site was that spot on the hillside which caught and echoed its eerie rumblings. I suspect it was the authentic voice of the horse, dragon or whatever the creature is supposed to be. One can imagine it reverberating across the countryside, the call of a god to his people, summoning them to worship, and the local references to a dragon may hold a clue as to the god's identity: for centuries the people of the villages in the Vale have maintained that the figure is a dragon.

47. Reading

The Reading dragons are stone figures on a capital which once stood in the Abbey Church, Reading, and is now in Reading Museum. On each of the four faces of the capital are depicted two dragons and two human figures. The dragons seem to be the same in each facet of the carving but the humans are different, and six of the eight are youths or boys. They are engaged in combat with the dragons, their mode of fighting being to try to yank the dragons' tongues from their moorings. In one scene they have been so successful that they have pulled out not only the tongues but the hearts and lungs of their adversaries. Experts who have examined the figures closely

34. The rather benign-looking dragons from the church of Charney Bassett (**48**).

Wantage Museum

have pointed out certain lines which are said to indicate that the dragons are intended to represent models, not real beasts. The humans, for their part, are clad in special gear which includes what appear to be hooves.

The interpretation suggested is that the carvings show scenes from a play, similar to a mumming play, in which a team of men and boys tackle the effigy of a monster. It could be a prototype of the miracle plays of the later Middle Ages. The dragons would thus be the forerunners of the later hobby horses, of which many examples survive. If so, they pre-date the earliest known hobby horses by some 200 years, for the first fixed date for hobby horses is 1389, whereas the Reading capital dates from about 1130. See also pages 15 and 30.

48. Charney Bassett
The dragons depicted in a sculpture in the church here are apparently water monsters, for they have paddles or flippers instead of hind legs.

WILTSHIRE

49. Avebury
The early eighteenth-century antiquarian, William Stukeley, thought he detected in the ground plan of the antiquities of Avebury evidence of former serpent worship. The Sanctuary, a timber and stone circle on top of Overton Hill, south-east of the main monument, he took to be the serpent's head. A winding avenue marked by megaliths links it with the great circle which he considered to represent the coiled body. A second meandering avenue leads south-westwards from the main circle to a group of stones near Beckhampton, and this was identified by Stukeley as the serpent's tail.

His theory is not entirely accepted, though it remains possible. Whether significant or not, the twelfth-century font in Avebury church has a carving depicting a bishop striking a dragon with his crozier. See also page 12.

50. Colerne
These two monsters, with snake-like heads and necks, may be seen in the carving on a cross-shaft in Colerne church.

51. Malmesbury
In the nave arcade of Malmesbury Abbey is a dripstone depicting a dragon with horns and a mane.

35. Some antiquarians have seen in the great circle of Avebury (**49**) an attempt to portray the coiled body of a serpent.

52. Knook

In the church of St Margaret at Knook is a sculpture of a Life Tree guarded by a dragon and a panther.

53. Salisbury

Salisbury Museum is the home of the Salisbury giant, who parades through the streets of the city on important festival days such as coronations and royal weddings. The giant has as a companion the Hob-nob, a hobby horse with snapping jaws who capers about on the fringes of the procession, making fun for the spectators. The giant, identified as St Christopher, was appropriated in the Middle Ages as the patron of the city's Tailors' Guild and as such paraded on Midsummer Day, 24 June, but earlier it is thought he may have been associated with St George's Day, 23 April. If so, this gives added significance to the Hob-nob, who resembles Snap, the Norwich dragon (**85**), closely enough to be classified as a dragon. The Hob-nob, wears a helmet and veil, and underneath his face is blackened, all in the interests of anonymity.

99

54. Quidhampton

In the still extant version of the Quidhampton mumming play, last performed in 1913, are several references to dragons. Two of the characters, King George and Bold Soldier, both claim to have fought with dragons. However, as these combats took place in foreign lands the dragons are not British. See page 24.

GLOUCESTERSHIRE

55. Stinchcombe

Nothing is known about this dragon, except that it once gave its name to a megalith which has since disappeared. The stone is mentioned in 1651.

56. Harnhill

The church has a carving of St Michael killing a dragon.

57. Deerhurst

The Deerhurst dragon evidently had a dual personality. One record (Sir Robert Atkyns' *The Ancient and Present State of Gloucestershire,* written in 1712) speaks of it as 'a serpent of prodigious bigness', which roamed the countryside feeding on cattle and killing people with its poisonous breath. Yet it is also a milk-drinking dragon, for it is eventually trapped by the offering of a vast quantity of milk. This was set out for the dragon by a local labourer, bearing the undistinguished name of John Smith. The dragon drank the whole lot so greedily that afterwards it was glad to stretch out on the grass, sunning itself as it digested its meal. Like a bird ruffling up its feathers when dust-bathing, the dragon opened out its scales to allow the air to circulate. John Smith, seeing his chance, attacked the dragon with an axe and, by striking between the scales, managed to cut off its head. He was rewarded by a grant of land on Walton Hill, which his descendants retained for many generations. An eighteenth-century member of the family still possessed the axe with which the fatal blow was struck. The church at Deerhurst reveals what are said to be portraits of the dragon, to those who take the trouble to look for them. They are the stone heads of fierce-looking creatures, one over the outer door and five more in the interior of the church.

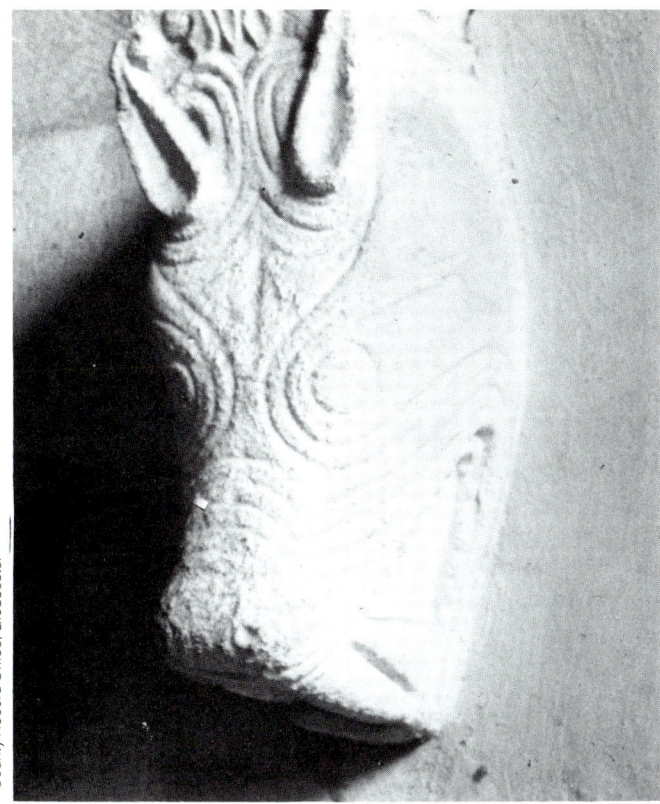

36. One of the six stone carvings depicting the dragon of Deerhurst (**57**) in the church there.

58. Quenington

A sculpture in the church here shows Christ rescuing people from the jaws of a dragon.

59. Stratton

Here a church carving depicts a Life Tree with guardian dragon.

60. Ruardean

In a church sculpture here, the hero who is slaying a dragon is St George.

61. Moreton Valence

The dragon depicted with St Michael in a carving in the church at Moreton Valence is apparently a water monster, for it has flippers or paddles instead of legs, and the long neck, small head and double humps associated with pictures of the Loch Ness monster and of sundry sea-serpents.

OXFORDSHIRE

62. Burford

Burford once possessed a dragon and a giant, whose effigies were carried in procession on important local occasions. One such festival was Midsummer Day, the feast day of St John the Baptist, who was the patron saint of the town; another was Whitsuntide. William Camden, in his *Britannia* (1586), says that a new dragon was constructed each year and was carried through the streets 'with great jollity'. His explanation of the occasion was that it celebrated the victory, in a battle fought at Burford in the year 750, of the King of the West Saxons over King Ethelbald of Mercia; the Mercian battle standard displayed a golden dragon.

Burford also had a mumming play, the cast of which featured a dragon. It includes two combats between St George and the dragon, in the first of which the dragon wins, in the second St George. See page 24.

63. Adderbury

Around the tower of Adderbury church are more than a hundred splendid carvings of mythical beasts and scenes from mediaeval life. The fantastic creatures include a dragon with a twisted tail, a gryphon, another dragon with one head and two bodies, and an evil-looking worm attacking a man. An archer who has drawn his bow at an advancing monster has hit an old woman by mistake. There are other fine carvings on the roof corbels inside the church, but no more dragons.

64. Garsington

A barrow at Garsington is known as Dragon Hoard. The name is first recorded in the thirteenth century. See page 45.

65. Kencott

A sculpture in Kencott church depicts an archer about to loose an arrow at a dragon.

66. Great Rollright

In view of the proximity of the Rollright Stones, a pre-historic circle of some seventy megaliths with a batch of associated legends, it somehow seems appropriate that the church of Great Rollright should contain a carving of a dragon devouring a human head, though there is no apparent connection between the stones and the sculpture.

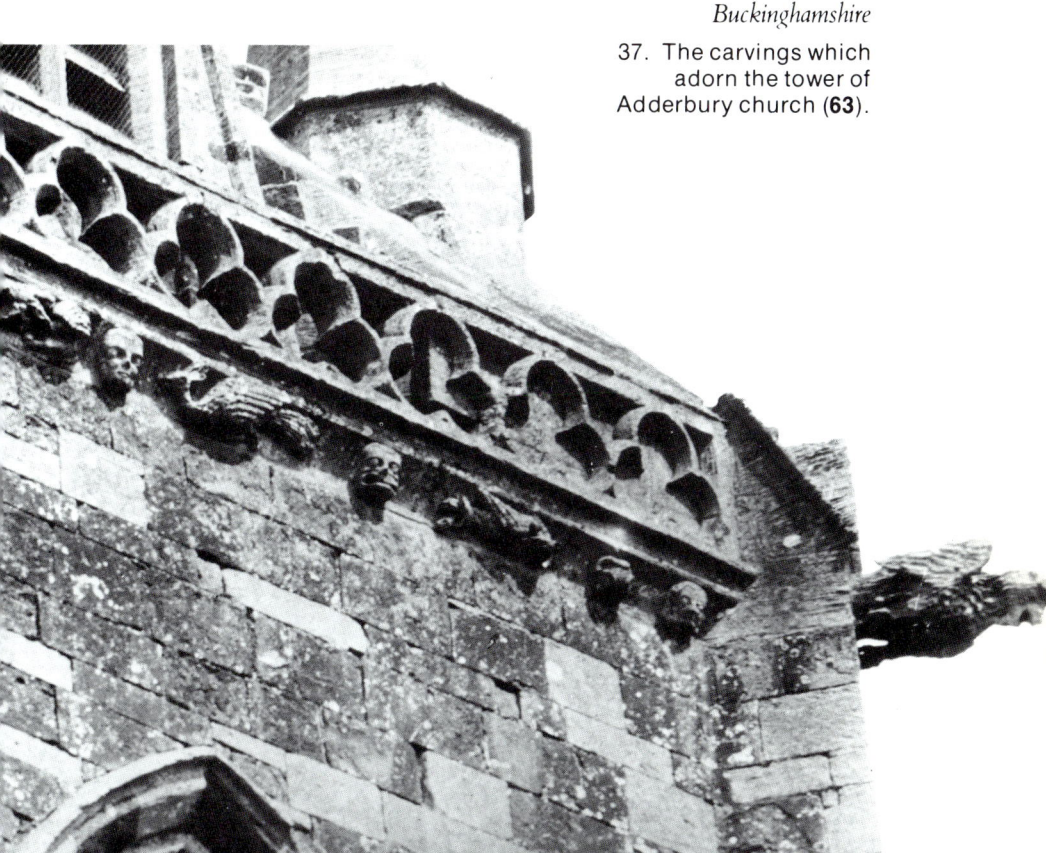

37. The carvings which
adorn the tower of
Adderbury church (**63**).

Banbury Museum

BUCKINGHAMSHIRE

67. Dinton

The space on a Norman tympanum in Dinton church is occupied by a dramatic Life Tree, a feature of which consists of two dragons standing under the tree and eating the fruit. At its base, too, a somewhat diminutive St Michael is confronted by a formidable dragon with two tails.

68. Leckhampstead

A sculpture in the church here shows two dragons fighting over a cowering human.

103

38. The Norman tympanum from Dinton church (**67**).

39. The Leckhampstead
dragons (**68**).

HERTFORDSHIRE

69. Brent Pelham

The story of the Brent Pelham dragon is one of the best-known of English dragon tales, perhaps because the dragon-killer was a popular local hero. His name was Piers Shonks, lord of the manor of Pelham and a man mighty in stature and exploits. He even managed to get the better of the Devil.

The dragon lived in a cavern under the roots of a giant yew tree, which once stood 'on the boundary between Great Pepsells and Little Pepsells fields'. After the manner of dragons, it went about creating havoc and terror in the countryside, to such an extent that it became a favourite of the Devil. Piers Shonks went out to do battle in full armour, bearing sword and spear and accompanied by three hounds. The battle was a straightforward slogging match, waged without Piers Shonks resorting to any of the ingenious tricks beloved by dragon-killers. In the end he won by thrusting his spear down the dragon's throat.

The story has a sequel. The Devil was so incensed at losing one of his favourite pets that he swore to have Piers Shonks' soul. 'I'll have him,' he declared, 'whether he is buried inside or outside the church.' Piers Shonks determined otherwise. When he knew he was dying he took his bow and fired an arrow at random. Where it struck the north wall of Pelham church he was buried in a cavity constructed for the purpose, so that his mortal remains lie neither inside nor outside the church. See also page 66.

His tomb may still be seen, surmounted by a black marble slab decorated with carvings of the chief characters of the story. To underline his triumph over the Devil, an angel is depicted carrying his soul to heaven. The dragon, watching ineffectively, is a two-legged monster with small wings, a massive coiled tail, large ears and a beard.

Attempts have been made to identify Piers Shonks with some historical person. He is said to have died in 1086, but the tomb was evidently constructed in the early thirteenth century, and a Peter Shank had a manor here in the fourteenth century. Beyond dispute the Shanks or Shonks were an important local family in the Middle Ages, and the ruins of the manor house where they lived are still known as 'Shonkes'.

The belief that Piers Shonks was a giant gained renewed credence when in 1861 his tomb was opened, revealing the bones of a man estimated to have been nine or ten feet tall.

70. St Albans

Early in the eleventh century Abbot Ealdred of St Albans, who succeeded to the office in 1007, set about rebuilding his abbey and used the ruins of Verulamium, the ancient Roman city nearby, as a stone quarry. In the course of the demolitions he 'flattened as far as he was able the den of the Dragon of Wormenhert, so dispelling for ever traces of the serpent's lair'.

Some two hundred years later the chronicler Matthew Paris, a monk at St Albans Abbey, mentioned the dragon in his book *Gesta Abbatum Monasterii Sancti Albani,* which recounts the history of the abbots from the earliest days. Nothing further is known about this very ancient but evidently important dragon.

71. Berkhamsted

A strange legend asserts that St Paul, visiting Britain, called in at Berkhamsted and banished for ever all snakes, dragons and thunderstorms! A painting of St George and the Dragon decorated a pillar in the parish church.

72. Tring

In the parish church a mediaeval corbel shows a dragon killing St George, rather than vice versa as in the usual version of the story.

73. Hatfield

On a pillar in Hatfield church a wyvern is depicted. It is a two-legged dragon, standing upright.

74. Bishop's Stortford

Bishop's Stortford had a dragon effigy which used to be taken in procession at religious festivals, such as Corpus Christi and Rogationtide. It was made of canvas on a wooden frame, concealing the men inside. It is first mentioned in 1482, when fourpence was paid to one Wyllm Northach 'for mending the dragon'. The dragon also participated in plays organised for providing funds for guilds and local charities and was let out to neighbouring parishes for similar purposes. In an inventory of church property disposed of at the time of the Reformation it is listed as an item sold but 'w'owte the assent of the parisshoners ther'; doubtless they thoroughly disapproved of losing their dragon.

A wood carving of the Bishop's Stortford dragon is still to be seen in the church.

75. Codicote
Though termed the 'Old Dog', the mediaeval wood carving depicting this legendary creature bears little resemblance to anything canine. It has a dragon-like body, a lion-like tail, a mane, the legs and cloven hoofs of a bull, and a monkey face with large ears. A chain is attached to a collar around its neck. Altogether it looks a fearsome creature, and a local belief that to pat the Old Dog will bring good luck suggests that few are brave enough to do so.

76. Bassingbourn
In the later Middle Ages, just before the Reformation, some twenty-eight parishes of Hertfordshire and Cambridgeshire, including the town of Royston, combined to stage a miracle play in the village of Bassingbourn. Whether this was an annual event or not is unknown, but the expenses of the production of a performance on St Margaret's Day 1511 are recorded in detail in the Bassingbourn churchwardens' account book. They include a dragon.

77. Wallington
A graffito of a hobby horse is to be seen on a wall of the church porch at Wallington. It probably represents an otherwise forgotten hobby horse who featured in a local religious play in mediaeval times. Maybe it was stored in the church porch or vestry.

BEDFORDSHIRE

78. Thurleigh
A sculpture in the parish church depicts a Life Tree, with Adam and Eve standing nearby and a dragon coiled around the roots.

SUFFOLK

79. Bures (Wormingford)
There is some confusion about the dragon or dragons infesting this area along the Essex/Suffolk border. To one of them both the little town of

Bures and the village of Wormingford lay claim, but there are other dragons which apparently have nothing to do with the dragon in the main story.

Looking first at the disputed dragon, we have a nineteenth-century translation of a document of 1405: 'Close to the town of Bures, near Sudbury, there has lately appeared, to the great hurt of the countryside, a dragon, vast in body, with a crested head, teeth like a saw, and a tail extending to an enormous length. Having slaughtered the shepherd of a flock, it devoured many sheep. There came forth in order to shoot at him with arrows the workmen of the lord on whose estate he had concealed himself, being Sir Richard Waldegrave, Knight: but the dragon's body, though struck by the archers, remained unhurt, for the arrows bounced off his back as if it were iron or hard rock. Those arrows that fell upon the spine of his back gave out as they struck it a ringing or tinkling sound, just as if they had hit a brazen plate, and then flew away off by reason of the hide of this great beast being impenetrable. Thereupon, in order to destroy him, all the country people around were summoned. But when the dragon saw that he was again about to be assailed with arrows, he fled into a marsh or mere and there hid himself among the long reeds, and was no more seen.'

This story, say the people of Wormingford, properly belongs to them. They assert that it was filched by Bures. The Wormingford version calls the dragon a 'cockadrille' and says that it was a creature brought back by Richard I from the Crusades for his menagerie in the Tower of London. After a time it escaped and made its way through Essex to the river Stour, where it settled down. Eventually it was killed in battle in a field called Bloody Meadows by Sir George de la Haye. The story is commemorated in Wormingford church by a stained glass window depicting the fight between St George and the dragon.

In this version of the story the dragon is described as having a thick body, short limbs with 'grete Nayles and Talouns' and a long curved tail. It sounds remarkably like a crocodile.

The Wormingford version would seem, superficially, to have the better claim to the story, for the element 'Worm' in the place-name should indicate a dragon legend. In this instance, however, it does not. The first recorded reference to the name gives it as 'Withersmundeford', which has nothing to do with 'worms' or dragons. Not far away, in another village, Little Horkesley, dragons are carved on certain beams and other timbers.

An entirely separate dragon story concerns a strange battle said to have taken place on the afternoon of 26 September 1449, in a marshy meadow on the banks of the river Stour near Little Cornard. A spotted red dragon from Ballingdon Hill on the Essex side of the river came down and fought with a black dragon from Kedington Hill on the Suffolk side. The battle was long but was eventually won by the red dragon. Both dragons were, however, able to retreat to their respective lairs 'to the admiration of many beholding them'. The source of this remarkable tale is a contemporary document now stored in Canterbury Cathedral. See pages 52 and 57.

80. Walberswick
Around the end of the fifteenth century Walberswick had a model dragon designed for appearances in processions and at religious festivals; there is a record of it being repaired and altered in 1479.

81. Ipswich
In the church of St Nicholas, Ipswich, is a cracked stone slab portraying St Michael fighting a very vigorous dragon.

82. Wordwell
Wordwell church has a sculpture of a Life Tree guarded by dragons.

83. Lowestoft
The order for the making of a new Wymondham dragon (**88**) in 1519 specifies that it was to be modelled on the Lowestoft dragon.

NORFOLK

84. Ludham
The villagers of Ludham were once terrorised by an aggressive dragon who flew over every night, making the villagers afraid to venture out after dark. Discovering where the monster had its lair, they blocked the entrance with bricks and stones, but the returning dragon soon disloged them. Then a brave and ingenious man found a single round stone that fitted exactly into the entrance hole and placed it in position while the dragon was away sunning itself. The dragon was naturally furious but could not shift the obstruction, so it made its way to the ruins of the Abbey of St Benedict, where it made its den in the vaults.

There, somewhat unsatisfactorily, the story ends. One feels that a dragon

40. In the vaults beneath these ruins of St Benedict's Abbey the dragon of Ludham (**84**) made its den after being expelled from the village.

left alive, even in the cellars of an abbey, would still be a potential nuisance, but evidently the villagers of Ludham were now free of it and they were not interested in anyone else. They retained an interest in their dragon, though, and sold models of it at their annual fair for a long time afterwards.

85. Norwich

No legends remain here of a real dragon. The famous Snap of Norwich was a character, arguably the most important character, in a pageant associated with the investment of a new Mayor in office. He last appeared in a civic procession in 1850, since when he has resided in Norwich Museum in the Castle Keep, so his structure can be studied.

Snap is made to be carried by one man, who supports the frame by straps over his shoulders. The dragon's body is barrel-shaped and formed around a horizontal pole, to one end of which the head is attached while the other, necessary for a proper balance, is the tail. The man inside is hidden by fabric drapes and by two small wings which are arranged to conceal his face. His hands are left free to operate the dragon's head and lower jaw, which are movable. The jaw, which works on a hinge, makes a loud click when it shuts; hence the name 'Snap'. The wings also are capable of being manipulated.

41. Snap, the celebrated dragon of Norwich (**85**).

Snap is traditionally associated with the Norwich Guild of St George, which was founded in 1389. On the feast day of St George, 23 April, the Guild paraded around the city with both St George and the dragon having prominent positions in the procession. Some accounts seem to indicate that during the proceedings they staged a mock battle. A modern author, Richard Lane, has made a careful study of the subject and has written a book, *Snap, the Norwich Dragon* (1976). He describes how 'St George rode on horseback and wore armour of beaten silver, beneath which was a colourful toga made of expensive material and trimmed with fur. He carried a silver shield painted with the arms of the saint...The horse was decorated in ribbons and laces, with red velvet for the cheeks of the bridle...With them was the Snapdragon.'

In the sixteenth century, though perhaps earlier, a new character appears. She is St Margaret, here identified as the maiden whom St George rescues from the dragon. The legend of St Margaret has its origins, like that of St George, in Asia Minor. She is said to have been the daughter of a pagan family, persuaded by her nurse to become a Christian. Disowned by her family, she became a shepherdess, repulsed the advances of a would-be lover and for that was shut up in prison. There she prayed to be allowed to see her adversary, the Devil, in corporeal form, and he obligingly appeared as a huge dragon, which proceeded to swallow her. He could not digest such a pure victim, however, and split in two, allowing Margaret to escape. Some modern authorities have identified all this as a moon goddess myth.

111

Whatever the truth of the matter, she became an important feature of the Norwich pageant, until the time of the Reformation. Then things gradually changed. The Guild of St George disappeared and the annual celebrations became 'the feast of the Mayor, Sheriff, Aldermen and Council'. The date was shifted from 23 April to Midsummer. The two saints were banished from the procession, but Snap was allowed to remain. He pranced around, enlivening the proceedings for the spectators, and, arriving at the Cathedral, sat outside on the 'Dragon Stone' while the service was in progress, as he had always done.

Through the centuries new effigies of Snap became necessary as the old ones wore out, and numerous accounts of the expenses incurred survive. A handbill issued in 1786 advertised that 'the old Snapdragon being dead, a young one is newly arrived here from Grand Cairo in Egypt, or somewhere else, which will make its first appearance.'

It is not widely known that the death-knell of much of the old pageantry of civic life in England was sounded by the Municipal Reform Act of 1835, which prohibited official pageants and processions. Thereafter Snap continued to make irregular and unofficial appearances in the streets of Norwhich until 1850, when he was pensioned off and given residence in the Museum, where he still remains. This particular Snap, the last of the line, was constructed in about 1795.

See also pages 29 and 44.

86. Costessey

This Snap is very probably an imitation of the Norwich Snap, which it closely resembles. Costessey, now a suburban village to the north-west of Norwich, staged its own pageant in the Tuesday of Whitsun week. It elected a mock Mayor who walked in procession with all his attendant dignitaries, on the pattern of Norwich. Breakfast was eaten at the Falcon Inn, five other public houses were visited en route, and festivities ended with a dinner and dance in a big barn at Costessey Hall. Throughout the proceedings the Costessey Snap capered about, snapping at spectators and devouring any coins they chose to throw at him.

87. Pockthorpe

This third Snap resided in a district of Norwich known as Pockthorpe. His particular trick was to seize the caps from the heads of boy spectators and then to demand a penny ransom. The boys used to dare him, darting as close as they could and chanting:

'Snap, Snap, steal a boy's cap.
Give him a penny, and he'll give it back.'

This Snap has now found its way into Norwich Museum, where it may be seen with the official Civic Snap. Recently a third Snap, origin unknown, has joined them.

88. Wymondham

A document of 1519 records that a new statue of St George and the dragon was ordered to be ready for the feast of St John the Baptist, alias Midsummer, the date on which Snap, the Norwich dragon, was also taken in procession. Wymondham is not far from Norwich.

HUNTINGDONSHIRE

89. Covington

In Covington church a dragon and a panther are portrayed in stone.

NORTHAMPTONSHIRE

90. Northampton

A dragon, together with a human figure, is the subject of a sculpture in the church of St Sepulchre, Northampton.

91. Pitsford

St George and the dragon are portrayed in a carving in this church.

WARWICKSHIRE

92. Warwick

A dun cow would seem to be an unlikely dragon, but some of the attributes attached to the Dun Cow of Warwick are distinctly unbovine. The

42. The dragons in Alveston church (**94**).   Shakespeare Birthplace Trust

discrepancies are probably explained by the fact that in certain parts of northern England the word 'kow' refers to dragon-like creatures. The champion who slays the Dun Cow, Guy of Warwick, performs some of his feats in territory farther north, so it is likely that in the Dun Cow legend we have an amalgam: the creature was originally a northern dragon or similar monster but, when stories relating to it were transferred to the Midlands, the local people were naturally confused by the name 'kow' and so embellished them with details appropriate to the cows they knew.

The outline of the story, as we now have it, is that the Dun Cow was originally a docile domestic animal. However, as she stood twelve feet high and was eighteen feet long, she produced a prodigious quantity of milk daily, enough to supply the whole countryside. Unfortunately a greedy witch once milked her dry, which so upset the cow that her character changed overnight. From being placid and obliging she became a raging monster, terrorising the countryside.

The champion who saved Warwickshire from her depredations was Guy of Warwick, a redoubtable hero who was a favourite of mediaeval romances. During an adventurous career he made two pilgrimages to the Holy Land, fought and won a number of exciting battles, including one with a dragon and another with a giant, and remained faithful to his wife, Phyllis, throughout it all. His combat with the Dun Cow, in which he was

114

naturally victorious, took place on Dunsmore Heath. Visitors used to be able to see the Dun Cow's shoulder blade at Coventry and one of her ribs at Warwick Castle, but the one has now been identified as belonging to a mammoth, while the rib is that of a whale.

One version of the dragon of Longwitton, in Northumberland (**179**), asserts that the hero who killed the monster was Guy of Warwick, thus linking this champion with the North Country.

93. Stoneleigh

Dragons, their bodies interwined, are shown in a sculpture in Stoneleigh church.

94. Alveston

The church of Alveston also has carvings of dragons.

WORCESTERSHIRE

95. Chaddesley Corbett

This dragon is portrayed in stone on a twelfth-century font in St Cassian's church. It has horns protruding from a horse-like head.

43. The font in St Cassian's church, Chaddesley Corbett (**95**).

R Hughes

44. Christ is trampling on two dragons in this carving in Pedmore church
(**97**).

96. Wolverley

A document of 1582 refers to 'Drakelowe' as a dragon site near Wolverley,
but no one now knows where it is or anything about the dragon.

97. Pedmore

Two dragons shown in a carving in Pedmore church are being trampled
underfoot by Christ.

98. Netherton

The Netherton dragon is the subject of a carving on the Norman tympanum
in a chapel of Netherton church. It is depicted as a fat-bodied worm, with a
long, forked tail, two claws and two wings. Nothing is known about it.

99. St Kenelm's

In the church here is a carving of four dragons, associated with Christ in
majesty.

HEREFORDSHIRE

100. Mordiford

This is one of the best-known of British dragon stories, made more
attractive by some of the graphic details preserved. For instance, when the

116

baby dragon was found wandering in the woods by a little girl named Maud it was an endearing little creature, bright green and 'no bigger than a cucumber'. Her apprehensive parents told her to get rid of it, but Maud hid it and reared it as a pet, feeding it on milk. As it grew it gradually revealed its true nature, hunting down first poultry, then sheep, then cattle. Eventually it became a man-eater. Though always remaining well-disposed towards Maud, it took to the woods, making its den on the ridge of Haugh Wood and following a path, still known as Serpent Lane, down to the river.

As its depredations became increasingly serious, the local residents took steps to destroy it, and there survives a whole range of alternative versions of how they set about it.

1. The hero was a criminal under sentence of death, who was promised his life and freedom in return for killing the dragon. Taking his sword, he tracked the monster to its woodland lair, found it sleeping and hacked it to pieces. The task completed, he cut out its tongue and took it down to Mordiford as proof.

2. The same hero lay in ambush in a cider barrel at the dragon's drinking place, the confluence of the rivers Wye and Lugg. When the dragon appeared he shot it with a gun, pointed through the bung-hole of the barrel.

3. The same hero concealed himself in a barrel which he studded with sharp knives and hooks, all pointing outwards, of course. When the dragon appeared he revealed his presence and the infuriated creature attacked, but it injured itself so severely on the cutlery that presently it collapsed, dying. Thereupon the hero jumped out and gave it its death-blow.

In all these versions the hero himself dies in the moment of victory, poisoned by the monster's foul breath.

4. The dragon crawled down to the river after a flood and gorged itself on a drowned ox. When it was sleeping off the effects of its huge meal, the villagers surrounded it and hacked it to pieces.

5. The hero was not an anonymous criminal but a member of a distinguished local family, the Garstons. This view is strengthened by the survival of a verse said to have been inscribed on the church wall next to a painting of the dragon and recorded by a local historian, Broome, in 1670. It runs:

> 'This is the true Effigy of that strange
> Prodigious monster which our woods did range.
> In Eastwood it by Garston's hand was slain,
> A truth which old mythologists maintain.'

About that time a family named Garston were prominent in local affairs and gave many charitable bequests to the parish. Their crest was a wyvern, a two-legged dragon.

It seems that this was probably the original version and that the stories of the anonymous criminal were concocted later, when the Garstons had departed and had been forgotten by the villagers. However, the basic story may well be much older, for Mordiford was once attached to the Priory of St Guthlac in Hereford, the arms of which included a wyvern. See also page 64.

For many years a large painting of the Mordiford dragon adorned the west wall of the church. This painting was evidently renewed at various times and seems to have been altered according to the caprice of the artist. John Aubrey, the Wiltshire antiquarian, visiting Mordiford in about 1670, described it as having four pairs of wings, but subsequently it was given two pairs of wings and two legs, which should identify it as a wyvern. In its final phase, completed about 1800, it had four legs and two wings and a long tail. This painting was erased in 1812 and not renewed thereafter.

There are also references which seem to imply that there was a carving of the dragon outside the west end of the church.

A sequel to the Mordiford dragon story is worth mentioning. In 1875 the rector found two of his aged female parishioners trying to drown two newts in the church font. They explained they were afraid the newts would grow up to be creatures like the Mordiford dragon and start the troubles all over again!

101. Brinsop

Brinsop is one of the places where the dragon was slain by St George himself. The Brinsop dragon was evidently a water monster, for it lived in a well in Duck's Pool Meadow and was killed in a field called Lower Stanks ('stank' being an old English word meaning 'pond'). A fine twelfth-century carving in the church deals with St George, to whom the church is dedicated, spearing the dragon.

Some students suspect that the story may properly belong to the neighbouring village of Wormsley, which incorporates the element 'worm', meaning a dragon or monster, in its name. It was the site of a mediaeval abbey.

102. Kilpeck

These dragons, carved in stone, are to be found by the south door of

45. The Brinsop dragon (**101**).

46. The sculpture around the south door of Kilpeck church (**102**).

twelfth-century Kilpeck church. Other figures in this elaborate sculpture include serpents, a phoenix, signs of the Zodiac and a Life Tree.

103. Shobdon
In a sculpture in Shobdon church a dragon is being overcome by the not unfamiliar stratagem of having a cross thrust down its throat. The hero here is Christ.

104. Wormelow Tump
A dragon is said to guard a treasure hidden in the tumulus known as Wormelow Tump, and another a similar treasure in Old Field Barrows.

GLAMORGAN

105. Penllin
It is said that many years ago winged serpents inhabited the woods around Penllin Castle. They were remembered by old people still alive at the beginning of the present century, who said that they were exterminated because of their propensity for raiding poultry farms. They were brilliant creatures, the old folk recalled. See pages 32, 47, 53 and 70.

106. Penmark
A similar colony of winged serpents apparently existed in woods near Penmark. An old lady testified at about the same period that her grandfather had once shot at and wounded one of them in Portberry Park. After killing it in a fierce fight, he and his brother skinned it and kept the skin and feathers in the house for a long time. She claimed to have seen the skin. It was said that buried treasure was to be found where the winged serpents were seen.

107. Cardiff
This serpent is said to live at the bottom of a whirlpool which forms in the river Taff at Cardiff. The corpses of persons drowned in the river tended to disappear, and so the legend arose that they were dragged down and eaten by the serpent.

DYFED

108. Trellech a'r Betws
All that is known about this winged serpent is that it is supposed to guard a prehistoric tumulus in the neighbourhood.

109. Newcastle Emlyn
The wyvern in this story was a fire-breathing dragon which took up residence in the ruined castle of Newcastle Emlyn. Clad in impenetrable scales, it had only one vulnerable spot, its navel (or vent, according to one translation, and a navel would seem a curious feature for a dragon to possess!). In order to get the monster to expose itself, a soldier threw a piece of red flannel into the river. As indicated in other Welsh dragon stories, red to a wyvern is like a red rag to a bull. The dragon went berserk and gave the soldier a chance to shoot it.

110. Castle Gwys
This cockatrice seems to have been a sort of wyvern, and not unlike the Wherwell cockatrice (**28**). It possessed, however, a very remarkable feature in having innumerable eyes, making it impossible for anyone to approach without being seen. It seems to have been fairly harmless, for we hear of no depredations. Instead of inventing sundry bloody devices to kill it, the hero had only to 'gaze on it unseen'. For some reason, his reward for accomplishing the feat was the title to the Wiston estates. Several claimants tried and failed. The successful one fastened himself in a barrel which was rolled slowly done the hill towards the cockatrice's lair. As it passed, the man peeped through the bunghole and exclaimed, 'Ha, bold cockatrice! I can see you but you cannot see me!' Nothing further is recorded of the cockatrice, but see also page 55.

POWYS

111. Llanbadarn-y-Garrag
This dragon, depicted in stone in the church, was apparently a water monster, for it has flippers like paddles on either side of its two-humped body. It has a long neck and small head, like the Loch Ness monster is supposed to have.

112. Llandeilo Graban

This dragon used to return to roost on the church tower at Llandeilo Graban. One morning it found another dragon perched on another pinnacle of the tower. Infuriated at this intrusion on its territory, it lashed out at the newcomer with its tail and immediately let out a howl of pain. The new dragon was an effigy carved from a log of oak but studded with steel hooks and spikes. The real dragon attacked furiously, then coiled itself around the intruder and attempted to squeeze it to death. The tactics were, of course, fatal to itself. An interesting feature of the story is that the dummy dragon had to be dressed in red. The hero of the tale was a ploughboy who thought up the ruse and got the local blacksmith to help him make the dummy dragon.

SHROPSHIRE

113. Bomere Pool

Although not strictly a dragon, the monster of Bomere Pool, a few miles south of Shrewsbury, is more than a fish, for it wears a sword attached to a belt around its belly. Attempts to catch it are thwarted by its cutting through the net with its sword. The story is attached to that of Wild Edric, a celebrated landowner of neighbouring Condover Hall, who is said to have fought the Normans for three or four years after the Conquest. Naturally he lost his estates when eventually defeated, and local legend maintains that the fishy monster of the pool is the custodian of Wild Edric's sword until one of his true descendants comes to claim it – Edric was supposed to have married a fairy maiden.

Incidentally, the pool is also alleged to have in its depths a drowned village, inundated in Saxon times as a punishment for mocking a priest.

114. Much Wenlock

These dragons are portrayed, in association with an ass's head, in a carving in Much Wenlock church.

STAFFORDSHIRE

115. Wednesbury
The only reference I can find to this dragon is a light-hearted rhyme (source unknown but apparently fairly modern):

> 'The dragon of Wednesbury churches ate
> (He used to come on Sunday) –
> Whole congregations were to him
> A dish of Salmagundi.
> The corporation worshipful
> He valued not an ace,
> But swallowed the mayor, asleep in the chair,
> And picked his teeth with the Mace.'

116. Ipstones
In a sculpture in Ipstones church two worm-like monsters are portrayed fighting each other.

117. Kingswinford
This is a dragon having the honour of being subdued by St Michael. The carving is in Kingswinford church.

LEICESTERSHIRE

118. Leicester
In the later Middle Ages Leicester had a Guild of St George which apparently held an annual parade in which, naturally, a dragon featured, as well as a hobby horse. The effigies of both St George and the dragon were apparently kept in the Guild Chapel of St George in St Martin's Church. The parade at which they appeared seems to have been a movable event, occuring on a convenient date between St George's Day and Whitsuntide.

119. Hallaton
In a church sculpture here St Michael is overcoming a dragon. Hallaton is a village which has kept alive a very ancient Easter Monday tradition involving first a hare-pie scramble and then a bottle-kicking match against the neighbouring parish of Medbourne.

120. Stoney Stanton

This dragon is shown, in combat with a panther, in a sculpture in Stoney Stanton church.

RUTLAND

121. Egleton

A sculpture in the parish church exhibits the familiar device of a dragon and a panther.

122. Ridlington

A carving with a similar subject is found in the church of Ridlington.

LINCOLNSHIRE

123. Castle Carlton

We owe to William Camden, in his book *Britannia* (1586), the earliest account of this dragon. 'Sir Hugh Bardolfe lived in Castle Carlton in the time of Henry I. It is said in a very old court roll that in the first year that Sir Hugh was lord of the place ther reigned at a toune called Wormesgay a dragon in a lane in a field that venomed men and bestes with his aire; Sir Hugh on a weddings day did fyght with thys dragon and slew him, and toke his head, and beare it to the kynge and gave it him, and the kynge for slaying of the dragon put to his name this word *dolfe*, and did calle him afterwards *Bardolfe*; for it was before Sir Hugh *Barde*; and the kynge gave hym in his armes then a dragon in sygne.'

This outline story is embellished by several further details of interest. The dragon was protected by triple-plated brass armour but had one vulnerable point, a wart on its right thigh. The battle took place by the sea during a thunderstorm, and a flash of lightning occurring at an opportune moment showed Sir Hugh exactly where to strike. The monster had only one eye, 'the size of a basin', in the middle of its forehead. It also had a 'long, scaly body, short iron-clad leg and lashing tail'.

In addition to the somewhat intangible rewards heaped on Sir Hugh by the king he was also given the right 'to take a horn of salt from every salt cart passing through his domain', as well as freedom for ever from certain tolls. See also page 62.

124. Anwick

The Anwick drake ('drake' here means a dragon, not a male duck) lived under a great boulder in a boggy field known as Drake Stone Close. A man trying to plough the field one day found his horses and plough being sucked down by a quicksand. At the moment they disappeared, a dragon flew out of the bog. Next morning, at the place where they had vanished, there stood a huge stone in the shape of a dragon's head. A belief arose that a fabulous treasure lay beneath the stone, so many attempts were made to raise it, but all without success. Sometimes when operations were in progress the dragon (drake) was seen to leave the lair.

The boulder is still there, though now split into two.

125. Walmsgate

A dragon is reputed to be buried in a long barrow near here. The original name may have been 'Wormsgate' rather than Walmsgate.

126. Wigtoft

New effigies of St George and the dragon were made here in 1534.

NOTTINGHAMSHIRE

127. Everton

Two dragons, with manes, are depicted in a mediaeval tympanum painting in the parish church.

47. A mediaeval painting in the church of Everton (**127**).

Nottinghamshire County Library Service

48. From the north transept of Southwell Minster (**128**).   Newark District Council Museum

128. Southwell
St Michael is shown subduing a dragon in a sculpture in the north transept of Southwell Minster.

129. Hucknall
St George and the dragon are depicted in a sculpture in Hucknall church.

DERBYSHIRE

130. Drakelow
This dragon must have lived very long ago, for it is mentioned in a document of the year 772 and is buried in a prehistoric tumulus. Nothing further is known about it, but see also page 45.

131. Derby
A carving on a ninth-century cross-shaft in the church of St Alkmund's is said to represent a dragon or 'Great Beast' caught in a net.

132. Winlatter Rock
There are two stories attached to the dragon of Winlatter Rock, near

Chesterfield, but, unlike most dragon legends, they are not alternative but consecutive. One is a sequel to the other, and both are recounted by Ruth Tongue in *Forgotten Folk Tales*.

The dragon was a personification of the Devil. 'He came out of the North and laid waste all the land.' Eventually he was challeged by a priest, who climbed to the top of Winlatter Rock and spread his arms in the form of a cross. The dragon made three attempts to move him, sending great tempests to make him lose his balance, but 'the priest stood so firm his feet sunk into the rock, and it held him up'. When the ordeal was past, pilgrims used to come to see the holes in the rock made by the priest's feet.

Long afterwards the Devil in the form of a dragon again visited Chesterfield and started to devastate the countryside. This time he was challenged by three young lads, brothers. The story of their escapade is a curious one in that at every stage except the final one they countered queries with a statement that runs like a refrain: 'One can't, but three can.'

They took a heavy bar of iron to the blacksmith and asked him to fashion a sword from it.

'You won't be able even to lift it!' laughed the blacksmith.

'One can't, but three can.'

They met a farmer and told him they were going to take the sword to Winlatter Rock.

'You'll never be able to carry it up that great rock.'

'One can't, but three can.'

At the rock they met a shepherd and told him they were going to set up the sword on the top of the rock.

'You'll never be able to do it.'

'One can't, but three can.'

They made the sword stand upright in one of the holes made by the priest's feet. Then at last they parted. One stayed with the sword. One ran to Chesterfield to call the men to arms. One climbed to the top of Chesterfield steeple, from which perch he could watch the sword, give warning of the dragon's approach and signal to the people down below to ring the bells.

It all worked like a charm. The tempest that the dragon raised died away when the lightning flashed on the sword. In the watery sunlight that followed, the great sword gleamed like a cross. The bells rang. The men of Chesterfield, well armed, converged on Winlatter Rock. They held their swords aloft, 'hilts upwards, like a forest of crosses'.

It was too much for the dragon. He took to his heels and bolted down the first hole he could see, which happened to be the Blue John Mine. There he may still be, for the mine is reputed to be bottomless.

133. Ashford
Dragons with long beaded tails are portrayed in carvings in the church of Ashford-in-the-Water.

134. Darley Dale
In the church of Darley Dale is a carving of a dragon fighting a panther.

135. Parwich
This dragon, in a carving in Parwich church, is being subdued by the Lamb of God assisted by a stag.

136. Swarkestone
A dragon depicted in stone in the parish church is being trodden underfoot by an unidentified animal.

137. Newbold
The Newbold dragon may have had a recent origin, for he and a hobby horse were associated with a sword-dance team which was active around the year 1900.

138. Winster
This creature was a snap-dragon, of the same type as the Norwich Snap (**85**), and was apparently associated with a morris dance team active in the early 1900s.

CHESHIRE

139. Chester
Chester's dragon was a civic character who appeared regularly in the city's great Midsummer show in late mediaeval times and perhaps in its Corpus Christi plays and tableaux in earlier centuries. It was evidently larger than the celebrated Norwich Snap (**85**) for it needed two men to carry it. In 1564 its companions in the procession were catalogued as 'four giants, a unicorn, a dromedary, a camel, a luce, an ass, six hobby horses and sixteen naked boys'. The naked boys, it is thought, were boys wearing flesh-coloured

costumes, and it seems that their role was to stage a battle with the dragon – that is, if the 'savages' mentioned in a record of 1608 are the same as the 'naked boys' of earlier chronicles, for in it we read that the dragon was 'very lively to behold, pursuing the savages, entering their denne, casting fire from his mouth; which afterwards was slaine, to the great pleasure of the spectators, bleeding, fainting and staggering, as though he endured a feelinge paine even to the last gaspe and farewell'.

In 1599 a Puritan mayor, Henry Hardware, caused all the effigies to be smashed, and substituted only a horseman in armour to ride at the head of the procession. The innovation was so unpopular that two years later a new mayor hurriedly restored the traditional pageant. During the Commonwealth the Midsummer revels were again suppressed, and at the Restoration a new set of effigies had to be made 'as neere as may be lyke as they were before'. One item of expense reads: 'For makynge new the dragon, and for six naked boys to beat at it, one pound sixteen shillings.'

The revival of the old custom did not last long, however, for there is no record of the Midsummer show or its dragon after 1678.

See also page 30.

140. Moston

The Moston dragon was a water monster, living in a swamp by Bache Pool. One day it seized a child at the edge of the pool and was about to swallow it when a local hero, Sir Thomas Venables, shot it in the eye with an arrow. Sir Thomas was rewarded with a grant of land, on which the fortunes of the Venables family were founded. The Venables crest shows a dragon with a child in its jaws.

A dramatic engraving in a book, *Ballads and Legends of Cheshire* by Egerton Leigh (1866), depicts a knight in full armour fighting a dragon which is infuriated by the pain of an arrow in its eye, but in fact no legends give any details of the battle.

141. Antrobus

The soul-caking play of Antrobus is essentially a mumming play, though usually performed in Antrobus and neighbouring villages around Hallowe'en. A dark champion fights with King George (St George), lies dying and is revived by a quack doctor with magic medicine. A character which is unique to Antrobus, however, is the Wild Horse, or Hodening Horse, who in some respects resembles a dragon, or, at least, the dragons which appear in the guise of hobby horses. See page 27.

49. The Red Pillar of
Llanrhaeadr-ym-Mochnant
(**142**).

T.W.HANCOCK. DELT.

CLWYD

142. Llanrhaeadr-ym-Mochnant
The destruction of this flying dragon was accomplished in the same manner as that of the dragon of Llandeilo Graban (**112**). In this instance, however, it was a megalith, or standing-stone, which was dressed in red cloth and studded with hooks and spikes. The megalith is known locally as the Red Pillar or the Pillar of the Viper.

143. Cynwch Lake
The wyvern (two-legged dragon) of Cynwch Lake, near Dolgellau, used to be seen sometimes on the shores of the lake and sometimes on the slopes of neighbouring Moel Offrum. It moved by a kind of arching movement, like a looper caterpillar, and left a slimy trail, like a slug. Apparently it made a nuisance of itself, for a character known as the Wizard of Ganllwyd determined to get rid of it and hired some archers for the job. Unfortunately, whenever the archers appeared the wyvern vanished. At last a shepherd boy named Meredydd crept up on it unawares and cut off its head with an axe. According to one version of the story, the axe was a magic one borrowed from the 'Monastery of the Standard', which is supposed to have been the ruined Cymmer Abbey, two miles away.

144. Penmynydd
This dragon was slain by the same ruse as was used to defeat the Wherwell cockatrice (**28**). An ingenious youth lowered a highly polished brass pan into its lair, and the dragon, seeing its reflection in the mirror-like surface, fought the intruder to the point of exhaustion, whereupon the young man stepped down and killed it.

On to this straightforward story another has been grafted. There is a prophecy that the dragon will bring about the death of the heir of the local landowner, a boy who is an only son. To avoid this fate the father sends his son to a distant country until the dragon has been safely despatched. He then advertises a substantial reward to potential dragon-slayers. The hero is a local lad who performs the task and is duly rewarded. It is now safe for the heir to return. He naturally wishes to see his fallen enemy, now reduced to a skeleton. He kicks it contemptuously, but unfortunately one of its fangs pricks his foot. The fang still retains its venom, so the wound festers and the boy dies, as prophesied.

British Tourist Authority

50. Under Nant Gwynant (**145**), the mountain in the background, two dragons – one white and one red – lay sleeping under the waters of a subterranean lake, where they were discovered by the magician Merlin.

145. Nant Gwynant

Nant Gwynant, near Snowdon, is the home of the original red dragon of Wales. Long ago it lay sleeping, together with a white dragon, under the waters of a subterranean lake in the heart of the mountain. The presence of the dragon was revealed by a boy, who by doing so saved his skin.

Vortigern, the first Romano-British king of whom there is any record after the departure of the Roman legions, decided to create an impregnable stronghold by re-fortifying an Iron Age hill fort on Dinas Emrys, near Snowdon. He was frustrated by the disappearance, night after night, of the building materials he had assembled during the day. His magicians advised

132

Airviews (M/c) Ltd. Manchester Airport

51. Glaslyn (**147**), where two climbers claimed to have seen a lake monster in the 1930s.

that the remedy was to sprinkle the site with the blood of a boy born to a virgin. A boy was duly found and was doomed to be sacrificed when he recounted this story of the two dragons. The lake was drained and, sure enough, there were the dragons. Waking up, they started to fight each other, and after a tremendous combat the red dragon was triumphant. The delighted king thereupon adopted the red dragon as the emblem of Wales, seeing in the conflict an omen that his forces would eventually defeat those of the invading Saxons, represented by the white dragon. The name of the boy according to one version of the story was Merlin, who turned out to be the most celebrated magician of all. Another version identifies him as Ambrosius, a celebrated defender of Britain immediately prior to Arthur.

146. Llyn-y-Gadair

Llyn-y-Gadair is a small round lake near Snowdon. At some time in the eighteenth century one of a party of men decided to swim across it. His friends waiting for him on the shore saw that, as he approached, he was followed by a 'long trailing object winding slowly after him'. To their horror, a water monster raised its head above the water, seized the swimmer in its coils and dragged him down to the depths of the lake.

147. Glaslyn

Glaslyn is another of the lakes of the Snowdon range. Here in the 1930s two climbers on the mountain, looking down, saw a long grey body with a pale head rise slowly to the surface of the lake and then submerge again. It was unlike any creature with which they were familiar. This lake is popularly supposed to be bottomless.

148. The Afanc

There is more than one Afanc. The creatures are supposed to live in mountain lakes and adjacent caves in Wales, Glaslyn being one of their habitats. An Afanc that is said to live in a pool near the summit of Snowdon was dragged there from Conway, where it had been making a nuisance of itself. It had to be banished in this way, even though the task of catching it, binding it with ropes and employing a team of oxen to drag it up the mountain was formidable, for Afancs are indestructible.

149. The Llamigan-y-Dur

This is another monster of Welsh mountain lakes. It looks like a giant toad but has a tail and wings instead of legs. Although presumably it can fly, it spends most of the time under the water, where it grabs fishing lines and tries to pull the fishermen in. It adopts the same tactics with sheep, its chief food, when they come to drink.

THE ISLE OF MAN

150. The Buggane

Although the Buggane of the Isle of Man is not strictly a dragon, it can change its shape at will and so may well appear as a dragon, though more usually it is seen as a huge ram or a big black bull. Bugganes often haunt ruined chapels and churches, thus discouraging any ideas of rebuilding. They indulge at times in fearful bellowing. A celebrated Buggane once lived in the old church of St Trinian, where, to win a wager, a tailor sat one night for as long as it took to make a pair of breeches, in spite of the threats and wrath of the outraged Buggane.

151. The Taroo-Ushtey

This fearsome creature, which is also much given to long bellowing, is a kind of water bull. Sometimes it emerges to feed with ordinary cattle on the coastal meadows, afterwards leading them to destruction.

152. The Cabbyl-Ushtey

Another creature capable of rapid metamorphosis is the Cabbyl-Ushtey, or Glashtin, though it generally appears in the form of a horse. Like the njuggle of the Shetlands (**193**), it coaxes humans to mount it and then gallops with them into the sea.

52. The church of St Trinian, in the Isle of Man, home of a celebrated Buggane (**150**).

Photograph by courtesy of the Manx Museum

153. The Nikyr
A terrible water demon, imported by the Northmen, the Nikyr once lived in reputedly bottomless mountain pools.

LANCASHIRE

154. Stand
An Easter play with a somewhat complicated plot, similar to a mumming play, was performed in the nineteenth century in the village of Stand, in the Fylde district. St George's antagonist is described as 'the dragon with the horse's head'.

YORKSHIRE

155. Loschy Hill

In a group of villages in the North Riding of Yorkshire there appears to be a multiplication of dragons, though whether the stories refer to the same individual or to several different ones is difficult to decide.

Loschy Hill, a wooded hill in the parish of Stonegrave, was the home of a particularly unpleasant type of dragon which was nearly invulnerable, for it was able to heal itself of any wound almost instantaneously. Apart from which, it was an exceedingly venomous dragon. Sir Peter Loschy, a famous knight of those parts, prepared for his combat with the dragon by covering his armour with razor blades. The dragon attacked him on sight and wound its coils tightly round him in an attempt to squeeze the life out of his body. The tighter it squeezed the worse its injuries, so it retired temporarily baffled, but its wounds healed straightaway.

In the second round Sir Peter kept the dragon at sword's length and struck many mighty blows. Bit by bit he lopped off slices of the dragon's body, whereupon his dog seized each fragment and ran off with it, out of the dragon's reach. So the dragon was gradually hacked to pieces and expired. According to one version the tactics were deliberate, the dog having been trained for the purpose. As the dog grabbed each piece it ran with it to Nunnington, a village a mile away, a journey which would seem unnecessarily exhausting.

The victory achieved, the knight bent down to pat his dog, which licked his face. Unfortunately the dog had absorbed some of the monster's venom, which it passed on to Sir Peter, and both fell down dead.

156. Slingsby

Slingsby, a few miles from Loschy Hill, has a dragon story so similar that it almost certainly refers to the same incident. The dragon was killed by the joint efforts of a knight and his dog, exactly as at Loschy Hill, and both fell dead at the moment of victory. However, here the hero is not Sir Peter Loschy but a local knight, Sir William Wyvill, whose family is known to have lived at Slingsby in the fourteenth century. The place where the dragon had his lair is identified in a seventeenth-century document as 'a great hole half a myle from the towne, round within and three yerdes broad and more'. The dragon itself was more than a mile long.

Both Nunnington (near Loschy Hill) and Slingsby churches have monuments associated with their respective dragons. Nunnington has a tomb bearing the stone figure of a knight, his legs crossed and his feet resting on a dog. It is alleged locally to be an effigy of Sir Peter Loschy, but antiquarians who have examined it say it is Sir Walter Leye, who died about 1325. Some have also identified the animal as a lion, not a dog.

The Slingsby knight also rests his feet on a dog, and the identification of the figure as representing Sir William Wyvill is probably correct. The Wyvills had a wyvern on their coat of arms.

For good measure a third village, Stonegrave, the parish in which Loschy Hill is situated, also has a dragon in its church. It is carved on a stone said to be of Danish origin, and a naked man with bow and arrow is shooting at it.

157. Kellington

Kellington seems too far from the Loschy Hill and Slingsby dragons to have a common origin, but there are similarities in the story. The dragon here was an enormous serpent which lived in a swampy forest, and the hero was a shepherd named Ormroyd. In his battle with the monster the shepherd was aided by his dog, and both died at the moment of victory.

For the alleged proof of the story one is referred to a very ancient stone, perhaps the lid of a coffin, in the churchyard. It bears the carving of a man with his feet resting on a dog; also a cross. Local ingenuity has identified the cross as a shepherd's crook and so claimed that the man must have been a shepherd. A field called Ormroyd Close is said to have been given to the shepherd's family by the grateful villagers.

158. Wantley

Wantley is a lodge about a mile from the village of Wortley, near Rotherham. There are several versions of its dragon story, in some of which the attributes of the dragon and the hero seem to have been confused. For instance, the dragon was a fearsome creature with:

> '...two furious wings
> Each one upon his shoulder,
> With a sling in his tail, as long as a flail,
> Which made him all the bolder.
> He had long claws, and in his jaws
> Four and forty teeth of iron;
> With a hide as tough as any buff,
> Which round him did environ....
> All sorts of cattle did this dragon eat.

> Some say he ate up trees,
> And the forests sure he would
> Devour up by degrees;
> For houses and churches were to him geese and turkeys,
> He ate up all and left none behind.'

On the other hand the hero, More of More Hall, is described as a man of huge strength and unpredictable temper. Once, when his horse offended him, he seized it by mane and tail and whirled it around his head till it was dead. Then he ate it.

The tactics adopted by More for the battle were familiar ones in dragon legends. He had a suit of armour studded with spikes, each five or six inches long. These kept the dragon from closing in, and so the battle was prolonged for two days and a night. But the dragon had one vulnerable spot, in the middle of its back, and when More landed a kick there with his spiked boot the dragon succumbed. An interesting detail of the story is that More wanted as his reward (before the battle, incidentally!) a fair-skinned, black-haired maiden of sixteen, who had to anoint him in preparation for the combat.

The verses quoted (first published in 1699) are supposed to be of ancient origin (though evidently after the introduction of turkeys from America), but are now regarded as a skit on a legal battle that occurred in Elizabethan times. More, the hero, was a lawyer hired by the villagers to present their case against Sir Francis Wortley, an estate manager who was oppressing them with unduly high rents or tithes. Later generations of villagers, however, were so sure about the dragon that they eagerly showed visitors the exact spots where its head and tail lay, and the well to which it came to drink.

159. Handale

Handale Priory, now in ruins, was a small Benedictine house founded in 1133 near the village Lofthouse-in-Cleveland. Nearby, at some unknown date, there lived an immense serpent who used to tempt maidens into a wood and then devour them. It was eventually challenged by a young man named Scaw, who tackled the monster armed only with a sword and who, after a hard fight, killed it. His reward was marriage to an earl's daughter whom he found in the serpent's cave and through whom he acquired vast estates.

A few interesting details of the serpent are recorded. It had a crested

53. The landscape near Handale Priory in which the Handale dragon (**159**) lived.

head which it reared up, breathing out fire, and it also had a deadly poisonous sting. A stone coffin in the ruins of the priory was said to be that of Scaw, and the wood in which the battle was fought was afterwards known as Scaw Wood.

160. Sexhow

Sexhow, a small place about four miles from Stokesley-in-Cleveland, was once visited by a formidable dragon who took up residence on a rounded hill, demanding the milk of nine cows every day. At nights it kept the villagers awake by its incessant snoring, and its breath was so foul that some persons who ventured too near fell down dead.

Eventually an unknown knight came to do battle. It was a hard but straightforward fight, but in the end the knight triumphed and then went on his way without revealing his identity. The dead dragon was skinned and its skin taken to Stokesley church, where it hung for many years. It has now disappeared.

161. Filey

The dragon of Filey lived in a ravine on the edge of which the hero of the story, Billy Biter, had his cottage. One misty morning he fell over the edge,

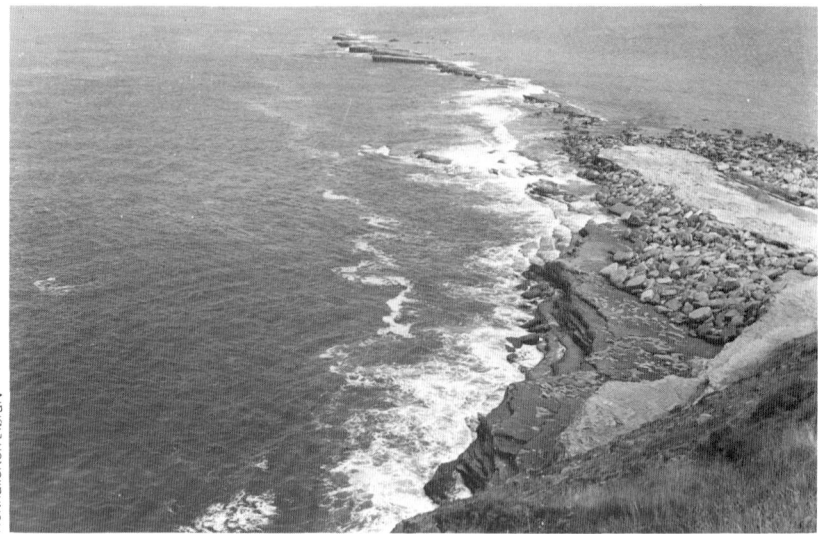

54. This reef of rocks, Filey Brigg, was once reputed to be the bones of the dragon of Filey (**161**).

right into the dragon's den. The dragon contemplated eating him for breakfast, but in his terror Billy dropped the parkin he was carrying, and the dragon ate that instead. Parkin is a Yorkshire delicacy – a sticky, treacly gingerbread. The dragon liked it very much and sent Billy back for more.

Billy was a hen-pecked tailor. His wife, disbelieving his story, took out the next parkin herself but, being drunk, she too fell into the gully, where she and the parkin were swallowed by the dragon. However, on this occasion the parkin stuck to its teeth, until the dragon was forced to go into the sea to try to wash it off. The townspeople, seizing their opportunity, armed themselves and followed it, preventing it from returning to land. And so the dragon drowned.

A reef of rocks, known as Filey Brigg, was said to be the dragon's bones.

162. Well
Well, near Ripon, had a dragon which, after causing considerable havoc in the countryside, was slain by a knight named Latimer who was a local landowner. A dragon appears on the Latimer arms.

163. Bilsdale
This dragon is known only through the name of a tumulus or barrow, Drake Howe, in which treasure is said to be buried.

140

164. Bishop Wilton
Several dragons are portrayed in the doorway of St Edith's church, Bishop Wilton, East Yorkshire, making a meal of some offending men.

165. Newton-in-Cleveland
Nothing is known of this dragon of Anglo-Saxon date, which is depicted on a stone in a buttress of St Oswald's church tower.

166. Austerfield
The church of Austerfield has carvings of dragons with certain cryptic signs.

167. Emley
At Emley the Life Tree depicted in a sculpture in the church is flanked by the Lamb of God and by a dragon.

DURHAM

168. Lambton
One of our chief sources of information about the Lambton worm is an old and anonymous folk song. It tells how the young heir to Lambton Castle, which is near Penshaw, when fishing in the river Wear one Sunday morning, caught a queer-looking worm which he threw into a well. Some

55. Lambton Castle, the scene of the celebrated combat in which a mediaeval Lord Lambton slew the Lambton worm (**168**).

BBC Hulton Picture Library

years later, when grown up, he decided to join a Crusade to the Holy Land and was away for seven years. While he was absent the worm, outgrowing the well, crawled out and began to make a nuisance of itself. To start with it seems to have been content with a milk diet, demanding the milk from a dozen cows for a single meal. Growing to an enormous size, it switched to carnivorous habits:

> 'This fearful Worm would often feed
> On calves and lambs and sheep,
> And swallow little bairns alive
> When they lay down to sleep,
> And when he'd eaten all he could
> And he had had his fill
> He crawled away and lapped his tail
> Ten times round Lambton Hill.'

There are several elements in the story of its death which are common to a number of other dragon legends.

The worm had the magical quality of being able to heal itself when wounded; even if it were cut in half the two ends joined together again. Several champions who tried to kill it were thwarted by these tactics.

Although lashing about with its powerful tail, the worm normally killed its victims by wrapping its coils around them and squeezing.

When Lord Lambton returned from his overseas adventures and learned of the havoc his thoughtless deed had caused, he realised that it was his duty to slay the monster. So he consulted a local witch – Elspat of the Glen – who gave him good advice. He was to stud his armour with spikes, thus counteracting the dragon's attempts to squeeze him to death. And he was to fight the battle on a rock in the middle of the river Wear, at a place where the current was strong. The reason for this choice of venue soon became plain. As Lord Lambton began to lop bits off the worm, the current carried them away down stream, so they were unable to join up again. The plan worked perfectly, and the worm was vanquished.

There is, however, a sequel to the tale. The witch told Lord Lambton that, in return for the promise of victory, he must take an oath to kill the first creature that came to meet him as he returned triumphant. The champion arranged that at a signal one of his dogs was to be released and, rushing to greet him, would qualify for the sacrifice. Unfortunately, his old father, forgetting the conditions in the excitement, ran down to the river bank and arrived before the dog. Grief-stricken, Lord Lambton was obliged to fulfil his vow. This is linked to the need to sacrifice after victory, and the story echoes that of Jephthah and his daughter, in the Book of Judges, Chapter 11.

It seems unfair that for this inescapable act of parricide he should be cursed, but that is what happened:

> 'On nine generations of thy race
> A heavy curse shall fall;
> They may die in fight or in the chase
> But not in their native hall.'

This was construed as meaning that for nine generations the Lords of Lambton would not die in their beds and, as far as it is possible to ascertain, the curse seems to have come true.

In some versions of the story young Lord Lambton, at the time when he caught the baby worm, was a dissolute, hard-living, hard-swearing youth with little regard for religion, as witness his going fishing on Sunday. The havoc caused by the worm was seen as a direct result of his wickedness and, having repented when he came to maturity, he was required to make amends.

Visitors to Lambton Castle may see a statue of Lord Lambton, clad in spiky armour, in the act of killing the dragon. Another statue is of a woman, said to be a witch. And the stone trough from which the worm drank his tribute of milk used to be on show.

169. Sockburn

Less is known about the Sockburn worm than about its relative at Lambton. Indeed, of the monster itself virtually all the information we have is contained in a manuscript in the British Museum: 'Sir John Conyers, knight, slew the monstrous and poisonous vermin, wyvern, asp, or werme, which had overthrown and devoured many people in fight; for that the scent of the poison was so strong that no person might abyde it. And by the providence of the Almighty God, the said John Conyers, knight, overthrew the said monster and slew it. But before he made this enterprise, having but one sonne, he went to the church of Sockburn in compleat armour and offered up his only sonne to the Holy Ghost. That place where this great serpent lay was Graystone, and this John lyeth buried in Sockburne Church in compleat armour of the time before the conquest.'

56. This weathered stone in Sockburn church portrays Sir John Conyers killing the Sockburn worm (**169**).

The Bowes Museum

The offering of a human sacrifice is similar to that in the story of the Lambton worm, though there it is of an aged father, here of a son. We are left to conjecture what happened to the boy. The phrase 'before the conquest' places the legend in Saxon times, and the Conyers family did claim a pre-Norman lineage.

The legend was kept alive by a ceremony performed throughout the mediaeval period and down to the year 1826. Sockburn occupies a tongue of land enclosed on three sides by the tortuous river Tees and lay on a much frequented north-south route. When a newly elected bishop of Durham crossed the river there to take up residence in his diocese, he was met by the lord of the manor who delivered the following speech: 'My Lord Bishop, I here present you with the falchion wherewith the champion Conyers slew the worm, dragon, or fiery flying serpent, which destroyed man, woman and child; in memory of which the king then reigning gave him the manor of Sockburn, to hold by this tenure, that upon the first entrance of every bishop into this county this falchion should be presented.'

The falchion is a broadsword, which is still preserved in the library of Durham Cathedral. It is decorated with dragons, lions and eagles from the Conyers coat of arms and has been dated to the thirteenth century.

The old manor house of Sockburn has been completely demolished. The ruined church of All Saints has a Conyers chapel which contains an effigy said to be of Sir John Conyers. He is wearing chain mail and is holding a sheathed sword, while at his feet a dragon and a lion are fighting. The date of the sculpture is the early fourteenth century. It does not therefore agree with the date of the sword nor that implied in the manuscript.

Historians attempting to rationalise the legend have suggested that the Sockburn worm can be identified with a Scottish raider, William Cumyn, who invaded the North in 1143, sacked the city of Durham and was eventually defeated by an alliance of local lords in which a Roger Conyers played a leading part. As a result, the Conyers were rewarded with the manor of Sockburn. But the date is too late, for the Conyers were there at least a hundred years earlier.

The Graystone may still be seen in Sockburn churchyard. It is said that a farmer once tried to shift it by dynamite but could not move it.

170. Bishop Auckland

In some respects the story of this monster is identical with that of the Sockburn worm. The worm was slain by a falchion wielded by a champion of a well-known local family, the Pollards. As a reward, the family was given a grant of land, which they held on condition that when a newly elected Bishop of Durham entered his diocese for the first time he should be presented with the sword. The falchion is lost, but the approved speech of welcome is preserved: 'My lord, I do humbly present your lordship with this falchion at your first coming here, wherewith, as tradition goeth, Pollard slew of old a great and venomous serpent, which did much harm to man and beast.'

This worm is said to have lived in an oak wood, which has led some writers to suggest that it was really a monster boar.

An interesting subsidiary story is told about the grant of land. The bishop told the victorious Pollard he could have as much land as he could ride around while he, the bishop, was at dinner. The ingenious Pollard thereupon rode around the bishop's castle and refused to give it up until granted a far greater estate than he could have otherwise claimed.

171. Durham

This may have been an exaggerated account of a real snake exhibited in the city. An entry in the register of St Nicholas', Durham, reads: '1568, that a certain Italian brought into the cittie of Durham, the 11th day of June, in the yeare above sayd, a very great and monstrous serpent, in length sixteen feet, in quantitie and dimensions greater than a great horse, which was taken and killed by special policie in Ethiopia, within the Turkes dominions. But before it was killed it had devoured (as is credibly thought) more than a 1000 persons and destroyed a whole countrey.' Our ancestors were evidently a gullible lot, delighting in marvels.

57. Hayes Water, in the Lake District, is said once to have been the home of a temperamental dragon (**174**).

Further dragons are portrayed in stone in Durham cathedral. Their coils help to hold in position a millstone on the bowed shoulders of a caryatid.

172. Hart
The parish church of Hart contains a sculpture of St George and the dragon.

173. Houghton-le-Spring
Two dragons are shown in carvings in the parish church.

WESTMORLAND

174. Hayes Water
This lonely little lake near Leighton Moss was the home of a dragon which shared the pool with huge char. It rarely caused trouble but gave due notice of an impending bad mood by churning up the water.

175. Long Marton
Dragon motifs occur twice in Long Marton church. By the south door is a

146

carving of a dragon being slain by St Michael; by the west door, a simple dragon.

CUMBERLAND

176. Burgh by Sands
The church of Burgh by Sands has a carving of the Tree of Life and a winged dragon.

177. St Bees
Here, too, the dragon is to be found in the church, where it is being overcome in a stone carving by St Michael.

NORTHUMBERLAND

178. Bamburgh
The story of the Laidly Worm of Bamburgh differs considerably from most. 'Laidly' is not the name of a place but is Northumbrian for 'loathsome' or 'loathly'. The word was used by a witch, a wicked stepmother, when putting a spell on a beautiful princess: 'A loathly worm thou shalt be, crawling among the rocks.' The story has been preserved in an old ballad, *Kemp Owyne*.

The witch in question was not a wrinkled old hag but a good-looking woman who had married the princess's father, who lived in the ancient castle of Bamburgh. She was, however, jealous of the lovely girl, Margaret; hence the curse. Only one particular knight could release her. In one version of the story he is named Kemp Owyne, but in another he is the princess's brother, Child Wynd.

In spite of her origin, the princess/monster assumes the typical habits of dragons. She devastates the countryside with her poisonous breath, so that not a blade of grass will grow within seven miles of her lair. Every day she demands a tribute of all the milk produced by 'seven streakit cows'. In one version she is apparently tethered to a tree by her hair, which is wound three times around the trunk.

Eventually the hero arrives. In the version which identifies him as Kemp

Owyne he is persuaded to kiss the loathly monster three times, on which Margaret resumes her former attractive shape (see pages 62–3). In the version in which Child Wynd is the champion he meets various obstacles on the way. He is overseas when he hears of the havoc caused by the monster and has to make a long voyage home. As he approaches Bamburgh the witch despatches a few covens of sister witches to repel him, but he counters them by employing rowan wood, which is well known to be efficacious against witches. Then a company of soldiers tries to prevent him from landing, and the worm makes things more difficult by lashing about with her tail. Bent on killing her, Child Wynd presently jumps ashore, but she is apparently able to communicate with him and tell him what he is to do. So he kisses her three times and she is a woman again.

The curse now rebounds on the wicked stepmother, who becomes a toad-like monster. She takes up residence in a deep well in Bamburgh Castle courtyard, where she still is. Some say she re-appears every seven years on Christmas Eve. She too can be released and resume her human form when a hero kisses her, but first he must unsheath Child Wynd's sword and blow three blasts on his horn.

Spindleston Heugh, or the Spindle Stone, a towering boulder on a cliff near Bamburgh Castle, is said to be the place where Child Wynd tethered his horse before he went to fight the monster. As in the story of the Lambton worm, visitors to Bamburgh used to be shown the stone trough from which the dragon drank its milk. The cave in which the worm lived has, however, been destroyed by quarrying.

See also pages 15, 17 and 65.

179. Longwitton

The story of the Longwitton dragon is a more conventional type. Here we have an evil monster who is vanquished by a hero in a ding-dong battle.

The dragon was a water monster, who one day appeared at three wells celebrated for their medicinal qualities. The wells are still there, in the grounds of Longwitton Hall, near Rothbury. In times past they were the scene of a traditional Midsummer festival, when people assembled to drink the waters.

The dragon was discovered by a ploughman, who came to quench his thirst. 'It had coiled its tail round one of the trees and pushed its long black tongue into the well and was lapping the water like a dog.' When it saw the ploughman it made itself invisible, but the man knew it was still there because he could hear it and feel its hot breath. Other people who timorously approached the wells had similar experiences. Mostly they could not see the dragon but could hear it and see the marks it made. Those who did glimpse it said it had a long tail like a lizard's, and a warty skin like a toad's. The usual allegations of wholesale havoc are lacking, and indeed the only complaint made against the dragon was that it kept people away from the wells. When a champion, a wandering knight, arrived at the village, however, the villagers were glad to hire him to get rid of the monster.

The hero happened to be the fortunate possessor of a magic eye ointment which enabled him to see the invisible. So in his first fight with the dragon he had the advantage, for the dragon, assuming that it was invisible, attacked without due caution. However, it too had a magic asset in being able to heal its wounds almost immediately, like other dragons we have met. So at the end of the first day the two combatants wearily retired with honours equal.

The battle was resumed the next morning and raged all day, with the same result.

On the third day the knight, carefully observing his opponent, saw that it would not move away from the well and realised that it always kept its tail in the water.

'That,' he thought, 'must be the secret of its strength.'

So, pretending to be exhausted, he started to retreat. The dragon, following him, was then lured away from the well and the knight, wheeling his horse suddenly, was able to get between the well and the monster. Although the dragon continued to fight desperately, it was now at a disadvantage. Its wounds no longer healed and presently it fell over and expired.

There is no sequel. The villagers of Longwitton bury their dragon, tidy up the wells and settle back to their normal routine.

180. Gunnarton Fell

This is a treasure-guarding dragon that protects a barrow on Money Hill on Gunnarton Fell, above the North Tyne near Chollerton and just north of Hadrian's Wall. No details about it are known.

ROXBURGHSHIRE

181. Linton

The Linton worm seems to have been a lethargic creature, for instead of rampaging about the countryside, spreading terror and devastation, it stayed in its den on Linton Hill and sucked its prey into its cavern. This was possible because its breath was so powerful that every time it breathed in, all the sheep and cattle within range were drawn in. After a meal it would crawl out and sun itself on the hillside, its heavy body creating spiralling terraces which can still be seen.

Its nuisance value being considerable, the local peasantry offered substantial rewards to anyone who would rid them of their worm. The champion who accepted the challenge is known as the Laird of Lariston; his personal name is unrecorded, though the Somerville family, who were Lords of Linton for several centuries, claimed him as one of theirs. The land and title came to them, they said, as a reward for his gallant deed, which was dated as 1174. The lord was also given the post of Royal Falconer to the King of Scotland.

The laird's strategy was ingenious. He fixed a lump of peat to a wheel attached to his lance, dipped it in boiling pitch, brimstone and resin, then rammed it down the dragon's throat.

The Somerville family crest includes a wheel and the figure of a dragon, and in Linton church is a carving of a mounted knight engaged in combat with two monstrous creatures. Some authorities, however, consider that one of the 'monsters' is supposed to be the Lamb of God.

KIRKCUDBRIGHTSHIRE

182. Solway Firth

A story of unknown antiquity relates how a monstrous 'sea-worm' came into the Solway Firth and played havoc with the fish shoals on which the people of the coast heavily relied. It was not averse to a meal of livestock and humans as well. In desperation the people erected on the seashore at low tide a palisade of sharpened stakes. Roaring as it came in on the tide, the sea-worm impaled itself on the stakes and remained there, bellowing in its death throes, for three days. Its carcass was eaten by sea-birds and fish.

This sounds like a memory of an actual event, perhaps the stranding of a large whale.

183. Dalry

The serpent of Dalry was an enormous white monster which wound itself around Mote Hill. Little is recorded about it, but evidently it made a nuisance of itself, for a reward was offered to any champion who would kill it. The hero was the local blacksmith who made himself a marvellous suit of armour, studded with retractable spikes. Wearing it, he employed the alarming expedient of allowing the serpent to swallow him. Once inside the monster's stomach he started to wriggle and roll about, whereupon the spikes tore the serpent's intestines until it expired from internal bleeding.

ANGUS

184. Strathmartin

This dragon is also known as the Pittempton dragon, the Baldragon or the Balluderon dragon, for the stone on which its demise is alleged to be recorded is situated in a field near all these places. Nearby, too, is a well called Nine Maidens Well, which is said to derive its name from nine maidens who were devoured by the dragon when they went, one after another, to the well to fetch water. One version implies that their fate was a punishment for breaking the Sabbath by carrying water on the sacred day. The dragon, who was evidently the guardian of the well, was slain by a young man named Martin, who was the lover of one of the girls.

The stone itself, with carvings of two horsemen, a transfixed serpent and a strange unidentifiable creature, is thought to be of Pictish origin.

ARGYLLSHIRE

185. Ben Vair

Two stories are told of the dragon of Ben Vair, near Ballachulish on the coast of Argyll. In both, the dragon committed the usual depredations until the local inhabitants were desperate to be rid of it.

In one story the hero is a sea captain, Charles the Skipper, who anchored his boat some little way off-shore and built a bridge of barrels, soundly lashed together, as a means of access. Bound into the fabric of this precarious bridge were innumerable sharp spikes. When the trap was ready, Charles the Skipper lit a fire on his boat and started to prepare a good barbecue. The smell of the roasting meat was wafted to the dragon in its lair, who found it irresistible. Leaping down to the shore, it started to cross the bridge, but with every step more and more spikes pierced its scaly skin. Arriving at the end of the causeway, it found that the captain had prudently left a wide gap between it and the boat. The wounded dragon had the strength neither to leap the chasm nor to retrace its steps along the bridge, so there, on the last bobbing barrels, it lay down and expired.

The second version of the story shows the dragon in a romantic and attractive light. It is a female dragon, with a brood of young in a cornstack on a neighbouring farm. Discovering the dragonets, the farmer set fire to the stack. Hearing the shrieks of her young as they were roasted alive, the dragon came hurtling down but was unable to save them. Overcome with grief, she beat herself to death on a great rock by the shore.

186. The Boobrie

This strange and fearsome creature was said to inhabit glens near sea lochs in Argyllshire. It was a huge monster, with a footprint as big as a cartwheel, and it preyed voraciously on sheep and cattle. Yet, oddly, it was said to look like a duck.

INVERNESS-SHIRE

187. Loch Ness

The Loch Ness monster undoubtedly qualifies for a mention in this book. It has a respectable antiquity, the first documented encounter with it dating back to the sixth century when it was seen by St Columba. The saint had requested one of his monks to swim across the river Ness to fetch a boat, but halfway across the monk was threatened by a sudden appearance of the monster. Seeing the danger, St Columba called to the monster to turn back, a command which it dutifully obeyed. On this occasion the monster was as close to the swimmer as 'the length of one punt pole'.

Since then it has been seen at irregular intervals. In the present century many attempts have been made to obtain clear photographs of it but,

58. Loch Morar (188), the deepest lake in Britain, is said to be the home of a mysterious monster that has been seen in recent years.

although several somewhat ambiguous ones have been taken, the monster remains extremely aloof when cameras are about. Since 1965 the Loch Ness Investigation Bureau has maintained a camp at Achnahannet for six months each year, and the watchers are now equipped with echo-finders, diving-gear and the latest electronic gadgets. Hordes of sightseers also flock to Loch Ness every summer, in the hope of catching a glimpse of 'Nessie'.

See also page 59.

188. Loch Morar

Loch Ness is not the only Highland loch to possess a monster. This twelve-mile-long lake is the deepest in Britain, having a depth of 1,017 feet, which is far deeper than the sea a few miles away. Evidence of the monster is supplied by two local men who were on the loch in their motor-cruiser on 16 August 1969. As they were idling along, preparing to make tea, a large and heavy body overtook and struck the boat. Then for a short time it lay alongside, and the men tried to push the boat away from it by using an oar as a lever, until the oar broke. One of them fired a deer rifle at it, whereupon it slowly submerged.

The observers described the creature as about thirty feet long with three humps which protruded about eighteen inches from the water. It had a flat,

153

snake-like head about a foot across. Its skin was rough and dirty brown in colour.

In the following year a Loch Morar Survey was formed and three of its members, including Dr Neil Bass, a marine biologist, were privileged to get a sighting of the monster on 14 July 1970. Another member saw it briefly on 4 August of the same year.

While the presence of a monster thus seems to be well established, there is insufficient information to determine what sort of creature it is.

See also page 59.

ROSS & CROMARTY

189. Loch Maree

In lonely Loch Maree is a mysterious islet, Eilean Maree, on which were a sacred tree and a sacred well. The islet and the Loch are said to derive their name from an early Irish Missionary, St Maelrubha, but folklorists consider that he has become confused with an earlier Celtic god, Mourie. Until the middle of the eighteenth century bulls were sacrificed on the island on St Maelrubha's Day, 25 August, and the local tradition was that they were sacrificed to the dragons of the lake.

SUTHERLAND

190. Cnoc-na-Cnoimh

The death of this monster was accomplished by almost exactly the same method as that used by the Somerville hero who slew the Linton worm (**181**). The champion here was a farmer named Hector Gunn. To fight the battle he demanded a spear 'seven ells long'. When this was provided he transfixed with it a great divot of peat, which he dipped in boiling pitch. Thus armed, he rode to meet the monster. In this instance the reek of the burning peat was so strong that the dragon was half-suffocated before the battle started. Writhing in agony, it wrapped itself around the hill where it lived – 'Cnoc-na-Cnoimh' means 'the Hill of the Worm'. Pressing home his advantage, Hector Gunn thrust the spear with the burning peat down the monster's throat and held on till it died.

Hector Gunn was rewarded with land and money by the King of Scotland; King William the Lion, who reigned in the twelfth century, is said to have been the monarch in question.

ORKNEY

191. The Stoor Worm

All other monsters are dwarfed by the gigantic Stoor Worm of the Orkneys, which was so big that 'there was no place for his body until he had coiled it around the earth. If the earth shook and the sea swept over the fields, it was the Stoor Worm yawning. His breath was so venomous that when he was angry and blew out a great blast of it, every living thing within reach was destroyed and all the crops were withered. With his forked tongue he would sweep hills and villages into the sea, or seize and crush a house or ship so that he could devour the people inside.' (Ernest Marwick: *The Folklore of Orkney and Shetland.*) What more could be asked of a dragon?

When this monster took up residence off the coast of Orkney, the king consulted a wizard, who advised that the only way to keep the Stoor Worm satisfied was to sacrifice seven young virgins to him every week. In despair, the people agreed to this tribute. After a time the turn of the king's only daughter arrived, and in an effort to save her he offered her in marriage to anyone who would rid his realm of the dreadful Stoor Worm.

Enter the hero, Assipattle. He is the youngest of seven sons of a well-to-do farmer and has a reputation for being a dreamer, his head full of romances and legends from the distant past. When he hears of the king's despairing offer, he realises that this is just the challenge he has been waiting for. The story at this stage is embellished with certain dramatic details, including a chase when Assipattle borrows his father's speediest horse to ride to the scene of battle, an account of how he steals an iron pot of glowing peat from an old woman, and another of how he steals a boat from a boatman.

Assipattle puts his plan into operation. Every time the Stoor Worm yawns, a vast tide of sea-water surges into his gullet. At the second yawn Assipattle in his little boat goes with it.

For many a mile he is carried through enormous tunnels into the depths of the worm's anatomy. Eventually, just as he is despairing of ever finding it, he discovers the monster's liver, recognisable by reason of its phosphorescence. With a large knife he cuts a hole in the liver and pushes the smouldering peat from the iron pot into the hole. Presently it starts to burn fiercely, and the Stoor Worm feels so ill that it retches and expels Assipattle in a flood of water.

The Stoor Worm shakes the world in its death throes. There are storms, earthquakes, tidal waves and volcanic eruptions. The Stoor Worm explodes. One lot of teeth becomes the Orkney Islands; another the Shetlands. Where its tongue falls, the Baltic Sea is formed. Iceland is formed by the remnants of its carcass, its still-burning liver and other organs being the Icelandic volcanoes. As for Assipattle, he is greeted with joy by the king, as he has every right to be. Her marries the princess and lives happily ever afterwards.

See also page 51.

192. The Nuckelavee

The Nuckelavee was a sea monster which was nevertheless usually seen on land, though not far from the shore. Its appearance was horrifying for, apart from having a huge lolling head, a vast stinking mouth and flippers instead of feet, it lacked a skin, so that you could see black blood coursing through its yellow veins, It normally appeared in years of drought and heralded an outbreak of plague. Altogether a nightmare apparition. It was also known in the Shetlands. See page 51.

Several sea-serpents have been reported from the Orkneys in times past. Ernest W. Marwick, in *The Folklore of Orkney and Shetland*, mentions four: one washed ashore on Stronsay in 1808, one seen near Swanbister Bay in the 1830s, one in Shapinsay Sound in 1910, and one off Fetlar in 1880. The first was identified as the carcass of a basking shark; the identity of the others is unknown.

SHETLAND

193. Njuggles

'Njuggle' is a generic name. Njuggles are the resident spirits or guardians of almost every loch or stream. They appear in different guises but most often as water-horses which tempt people to ride them. Once a human is safely astride, they gallop to the nearest water and plunge in.

59. The rocky coast of Shetland, the reputed home of njuggles, the Brigdi and other sea monsters (**193–4**).

A particularly effective njuggle once lived in a cave in Fitful Head and was tamed by a fierce character known as Black Eric. The njuggle, whose name was Tangie, assisted his master and the pair of them became almost invincible. At last a hero cornered Black Eric on Fitful Head and toppled him over the cliff, but Tangie remained at large to keep the neighbourhood in a proper state of apprehension.

The water reservoir of the town of Scalloway is known as Njugal's Water, commemorating a njuggle who once lived there.

Modern njuggles are said to have developed a wheel-like tail, to increase their speed.

See also page 51.

194. The Brigdi
The Brigdi was a huge sea monster which sometimes chased fishing boats and even smashed them. It has not been seen in recent years.

Bibliography

Balfour, M. C., *Country Folk-lore LV: Northumberland,*1904.

Beddington, W. G., and Christy, E. B., *It Happened in Hampshire,* 1937.

Boase, Wendy, *The Folklore of Hampshire and the Isle of Wight,* 1976.

Bord, Janet & Colin, *Mysterious Britain,* 1972.

Briggs, Katherine, *A Dictionary of British Folk Tales,* 1970.

Briggs, Katherine, *The Folklore of the Cotswolds,* 1974.

Camden, William, *Britannia,* 1586.

Carrington, Richard, *Mermaids and Mastodons,* 1956.

Cawte, E. C., *Ritual Animal Disguise,* 1978.

Collman, M., *Hants and Dorset's Folklore & Legends,* 1975.

Costello, Peter, *In Search of Lake Monsters,* 1974.

Costello, Peter, *The Magic Zoo,* 1979.

Deane, Tony, and Shaw, Tony, *The Folklore of Cornwall,* 1975.

Dinsdale, Tim, *Loch Ness Monster,* 1976.

Frazer, J. G., *The Golden Bough,* 1922.

Gee, H. L., *Folk Tales of Yorkshire,* 1952.

Grinsell, L. V., *The Folklore of Prehistoric Sites in Britain,* 1976.

Henderson, William, *Folklore of the Northern Counties,* 1866.

Hitching, Francis, *The World Atlas of Mysteries,* 1981.

Hogarth, Peter, with Clery, Val, *Dragons,* 1979.

Hole, Christina, *English Custom and Usage,* 1941.

Holiday, F. W., *The Dragon and the Disc,* 1973.

Huxley, Francis, *The Dragon,* 1979.

Jones-Baker, Doris, *The Folklore of Hertfordshire,* 1977.

Lane, R., *Snap, The Norwich Dragon,* 1976.

Lawrence, B., *Somerset Legends,* 1973.

Lofthouse, Jessica, *North Country Folklore,*1976.

Marples, M., *White Horses and Other Hill Figures,* 1949.

Marwick, Ernest, *The Folklore of Orkney and Shetland,* 1975.

Merrill, John, *Legends and Folklore, The Midlands,* 1974.

Michell, J., *The Flying Saucer Vision,* 1967.

Newman, Paul, *The Hill of the Dragon,* 1979.

Palmer, Kingsley, *The Folklore of Somerset,* 1976.

Palmer, Roy, *The Folklore of Warwickshire,* 1976.

Readers Digest, *Folklore, Myths and Legends of Britain,* 1973.

Simpson, Jacqueline, *The Folklore of Sussex,* 1973.

Simpson, Jacqueline, *The Folklore of the Welsh Border,* 1976.

Simpson, Jacqueline, *British Dragons,* 1981.

Southern, Richard, *The Seven Ages of the Theatre,* 1962.

Tongue, R., *Somerset Folklore,* 1965.

Toulson, Shirley, *The Winter Solstice,* 1981.

Udal, J. S., *Dorsetshire Folklore,* 1922.

Velikovsky, Immanuel, *Worlds In Collision,* 1950.

Welfare, Simon, and Fairley, John, *Arthur C. Clarke's Mysterious World,* 1980.

Whitlock, Ralph, *The Everyday Life of the Maya,* 1976.

Whitlock, Ralph, *The Folklore of Wiltshire,* 1976.

Whitlock, Ralph, *The Folklore of Devon,* 1976.

Whitlock, Ralph, *In Search of Lost Gods,* 1979.

Index

Bold figures refer to dragon numbers in the Gazetteer (pages 71–157). Figures in normal type are additional page-references.